CREATIVE

Paint ○ Print ○ Stitch ○ Stamp ○ Embellish

MIXED MEDIA

SHERRILL KAHN

Martingale®
& COMPANY

Creative Mixed Media:
Paint Print Stitch Stamp Embellish
© 2010 by Sherrill Kahn

Martingale®
& COMPANY

Martingale & Company
20205 144th Ave. NE
Woodinville, WA 98072-8478 USA
www.martingale-pub.com

Printed in China
15 14 13 12 11 10   8 7 6 5 4 3 2 1

Library of Congress Cataloging-in-Publication Data is available upon request

ISBN: 978-1-56477-948-9

CREDITS

President & CEO: Tom Wierzbicki
Editor in Chief: Mary V. Green
Managing Editor: Tina Cook
Technical Editor: Dawn Anderson
Copy Editor: Sheila Chapman Ryan
Design Director: Stan Green
Production Manager: Regina Girard
Cover & Text Designer: Stan Green
Photographer: Brent Kane

MISSION STATEMENT

Dedicated to providing quality products and service to inspire creativity.

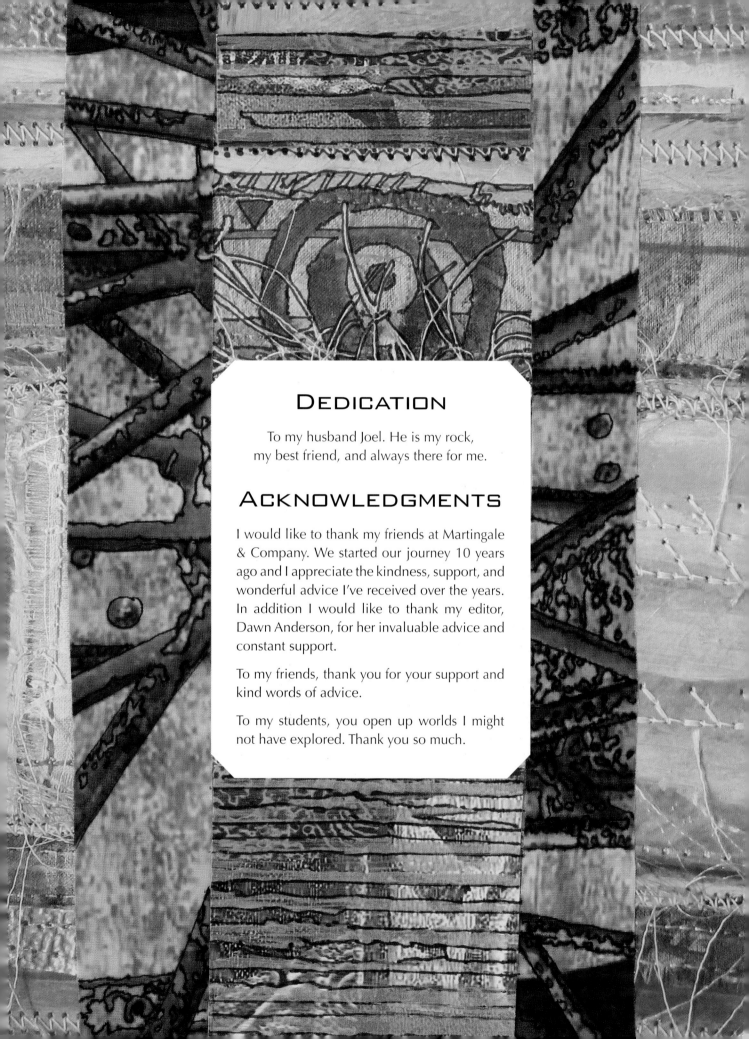

DEDICATION

To my husband Joel. He is my rock,
my best friend, and always there for me.

ACKNOWLEDGMENTS

I would like to thank my friends at Martingale
& Company. We started our journey 10 years
ago and I appreciate the kindness, support, and
wonderful advice I've received over the years.
In addition I would like to thank my editor,
Dawn Anderson, for her invaluable advice and
constant support.

To my friends, thank you for your support and
kind words of advice.

To my students, you open up worlds I might
not have explored. Thank you so much.

CONTENTS

INTRODUCTION

I *loved* writing this book. It was a journey of discovery. I experimented with common products that we use every day and found fascinating new uses for them. A walk through a local store yielded cosmetic cotton pads, facial wipes, baby wipes, hair gel, gelatin, and children's glue, all of which became tools for creativity. Shower mats, kitchen mats, and plastic place mats from the discount store became instruments for making prints and rubbings. In home-improvement stores and dollar stores, I found all sorts of items to use in art projects. These finds made me realize that anything is possible if you're open to experimenting.

Look around your home for items that could be used in a new way. Think outside the box, as I did when I used my electric griddle for a melted-crayon technique. Through experimentation, your work will grow and you'll have great fun in the process.

In addition to loads of techniques for creating unique artwork, I've included chapters on making backgrounds and on composing good designs. The ideas presented are meant to be used not only with the techniques in this book, but with all your artwork.

As you create, remember to have fun, as I did while writing this book.

TOOLS AND SUPPLIES

Here you'll learn about the tools and supplies used to create the artwork in this book.

For convenience, items are listed alphabetically in one comprehensive section rather than with each technique. When reading the instructions for the techniques covered in this book, refer back to this list. Only a few of the supplies will be needed for each technique. Begin collecting the materials for the projects that appeal to you most, and add more tools and supplies over time.

Aluminum foil. Extra-heavy aluminum foil is used to cover the surface of an electric griddle when creating designs with melted crayons or Dorland's Wax Medium.

Applicator bottles and tips. Use a metal applicator tip with plastic applicator-tipped paint bottles to produce fine paint lines.

Ballpoint pen. A ballpoint pen works well for adding designs to craft foam when making craft-foam stamps.

Bone folder. A bone folder is used for pressing fabric securely to inkjet labels in preparation for printing on fabric.

Brayer. Use a hard 4"-wide brayer to apply paint for creative effects.

Brushes. Use 1"- and ½"-wide flat brushes for applying paint or glue. Use a #2 detail brush for painting fine lines.

Candle. A white candle can be melted along with crayons to create unique patterns on a design surface. Do not use paraffin candles for this purpose because paraffin can smoke.

Cardboard. Corrugated cardboard is a great base material to adhere craft-foam shapes to when making creative foam stamps (see page 83). It can also be used as a textual surface when making rubbings with crayon.

Containers. Small white cups work well for mixing paints. A shallow water container is helpful for wetting fabrics.

Cotton pads. Cosmetic cotton pads dye well and can be used as embellishments in collages.

Crayons. All kinds of crayons can be used for creative techniques. Try regular waxed, metallic, glitter, soy-based, or any other kind.

Cuttlebug and accessories. Provo Craft's Cuttlebug, dies, alphabets, and embossing folders can be used to make embossed paper and die-cut images for use in a variety of creative projects.

Digital images. I often print photos to use as a base for my collage work. Sometimes I use photos of objects or people. Often I use photos of my previously created artwork.

Dorland's Wax Medium. This product can be added to paints to produce interesting effects— the wax makes the paint textured and transparent (see page 107).

Electric griddle. A pancake griddle provides a great heating surface for melted crayon techniques and for painting with Dorland's Wax Medium.

Eyedroppers. These work well for applying dyes such as Dye-na-Flow to the selected design surface.

Fabric. White high-thread-count cotton fabric and inexpensive habotai silk fabric accept paints and dyes easily. Tear the fabrics to the desired size. I often cut my fabrics into 12" squares. I also use Jacquard ExtravOrganza, Jacquard Silk, and Jacquard Cotton inkjet fabrics. Silk scarves can also be painted. Use the painted fabrics for collage backgrounds and cut or tear the painted fabric into smaller pieces to use for collage layers.

Facial wipes. Rinse facial wipes thoroughly to remove the cleaning agents, and then dye them for use in collages. Some have interesting textures, and they can be torn to create interesting edges. Each brand of facial wipe has a different texture.

Foam sheets. Adhesive-backed foam sheets can be used to make wonderful foam stamps (see page 83).

Freezer paper. Freezer paper is a good choice for covering your work surface. It also makes a great paint palette.

Gelatin. Use unflavored gelatin to create a unique printing block. See "Gelatin Printing" (page 101).

Gloves. Wear rubber or vinyl gloves to protect hands when working with dyes.

Glue. Glue sticks and washable white glue work well for attaching many collage elements. Washable white glue or gel glue can be used as a resist as well. See "Washable Glue Batik" (page 97).

Hair gel. This product can be combined with paint to produce interesting resists and creative effects.

Inkjet labels. I use 8½" x 11" labels to back fabrics so they can be fed through a printer to make prints. I also like to print digital images on labels and use them in collages. Labels can also be painted for use in collages.

Iron and ironing board. Use an iron and ironing board for heat setting painted fabrics between Teflon pressing sheets.

Markers. Use Sharpie permanent markers with fine and ultra-fine tips for adding waterproof details and color to projects.

Medium. Use matte or gloss medium to seal and protect some types of artwork. I sometimes use mediums when making facial-wipe and cosmetic-cotton-pad embellishments. It also works well for sealing digital prints printed with nonpermanent ink.

Needles. Hand-sewing needles are needed for adding stitches to fabric and paper projects. For machine sewing, use a needle appropriate for the thread type used in your sewing machine.

Oil pastels. These can be used to add color to paper or fabric. Oil pastels work great when used for rubbings. See "Crayons and Oil Pastels" (page 41).

Paint. All of the projects in this book were done with Jacquard acrylic-based paints. I used Versatex Screen Printing ink or Jacquard Professional Grade Screen Printing ink for gelatin printing. I used Neopaque when I needed thick paint. Where dyes and inks are called for, I used Dye-na-Flow; it is gorgeous on silk and heat sets with an iron. I used Textile Traditionals for colored glazes over previously painted work and Lumiere for all of the metallic paint used on the projects. You can also use water-based acrylic tube paint, acrylic paints in a jar, acrylic dyes, and acrylic inks of your choice. I like Jacquard paints because the colors are richly pigmented and dilute beautifully with water.

Paint palette. Use freezer paper or wax paper as a paint palette; I prefer freezer paper.

Palette knife. Mix paints (or hair gel and paint) together on a paint palette using a palette knife.

Paper towels. These will be needed for general clean up.

Paper. A wide variety of papers work well with paints and other mediums. Some of the papers I frequently use include cardstock, hot-pressed watercolor paper, copy paper, delicatessen paper, photo paper, rice paper, Bristol board, and white tissue paper. Use a large piece of inexpensive paper to cover the work surface (the paper will become covered with paint as you work, and then can be used for collage later). The paper should be at least 60# or more. I also like to use delicatessen paper or freezer paper to cover the work surface when working on small painted projects.

Pencils and sharpener. Colored pencils come in many forms—student grade, artist grade, soft, hard, thick lead, thin lead, water soluble, oil based, mechanical, and in roll-up plastic holders. I use them on paper, fabric, inkjet images, and just about any other place where they will adhere.

Plastic. Use plastic for covering your work surface when working with Dye-na-Flow, liquid paint, or ink to prevent staining.

Pressing sheets. To heat set painted fabrics, oil pastels, crayon work, and Dorland's Wax pieces, place the pieces between two sheets of delicatessen paper first, and then place them between Teflon pressing sheets. Follow the paint manufacturer's instructions for the length of time required for heat setting the paints on fabric or fiber pieces.

Rubber stamps. Rubber stamps can be used for adding visual texture and designs to creative projects. All the stamps used in this book are from Impress Me rubber stamps.

Rubbing plates. Plastic commercial rubbing plates are used to make rubbings with crayons and also for creating patterns using paint and a brayer. In addition to commercial rubbing plates, try using other flat textural items, such as bath mats, kitchen-sink mats, sequin waste, corrugated cardboard, rubber stamps, or textured plastic place mats.

Salt. I use Jacquard Silk Salt, but rock salt or other large-grained salt works well for creating patterns with a wet-into-wet technique. Do not use table salt because it's difficult to remove after it dries.

Scissors. You may need a variety of scissors including cloth, paper, and utility scissors.

Scraping tools. Combs, credit cards, and plastic take-out knives work well for creating textural patterns when working with paint and hair gel. See "Hair-Gel Resist" (page 91). I also like to create texture using a plastic spreader with notches on all sides, typically used for tile installation. These can be found in home improvement stores.

Scrub brush. Use a scrub brush to remove glue when doing washable glue batik (see page 97) and also to clean your hands after working with paint.

Sewing machine. I use a sewing machine for stitching some of my collage elements to design surfaces and frequently use stitching with variegated thread to embellish my artwork. I use a Janome 6600 or a Janome Jem.

Sponge squares. Use sponge squares for applying paint to rubber stamps and to the design surface. Purchase a large, non-hardening sponge from a home improvement store, and then cut it into 1½" squares. You will generally find the sponges in the tile, wallpaper, or paint department. The sponges are dark yellow in color. I use sponges more than any other tool to apply paint to the surface.

Spatula. Use a wooden spatula to hold the design surface in place when working with melted crayon or Dorland's Wax Medium on an electric griddle.

Spray bottle. A fine-mist spray bottle works well for dampening the design surface when working with wet techniques.

Thread. You'll need thread for machine and hand stitching. I often use variegated thread, as it adds further interest to the design.

Toothbrush. Use a battery-operated rotary toothbrush for applying paint to a design surface and for cleaning rubber stamps.

X-Acto knife and self-healing cutting mat. Use for cutting paper and for cutting stencil designs in playing cards.

Yarns and threads. Decorative yarns and threads can add texture and color to a design surface. I used them to add texture to cosmetic cotton pad embellishments and for embellishing some of the finished gallery pieces.

Dorland's Wax Medium was mixed with paint to create this composition on fabric. See page 107 for more information.

CREATING IMAGINATIVE BACKGROUNDS FOR YOUR COMPOSITIONS

Painted backgrounds make a great base for collage or other creative work. You can also cut or tear painted surfaces into pieces to make appliqués or other collage elements. In addition to the techniques presented below, see "Brayer Techniques" (page 55) for another great way to paint a background surface.

When painting, I protect my work surface with delicatessen paper. Some paint gets onto the deli paper during the creative process, giving me a new design that can be further embellished and incorporated into future designs. When using dyes, cover the work surface with plastic first and lay the deli paper over the plastic, to prevent staining.

WET-INTO-WET BACKGROUNDS

This technique is done with Dye-na-Flow, so be sure to cover the work surface with plastic. It is also a good idea to wear protective gloves.

1. Sponge water onto the design surface. If using cardstock, sponge water onto both the front and back of the surface to prevent buckling.

2. Apply liquid paint, such as Dye-na-Flow, to the surface using an applicator bottle or eye dropper. The color should bleed at the edges.

3. Apply additional liquid-paint colors to the surface as desired until satisfied with the result.

4. Spray additional water onto the surface.

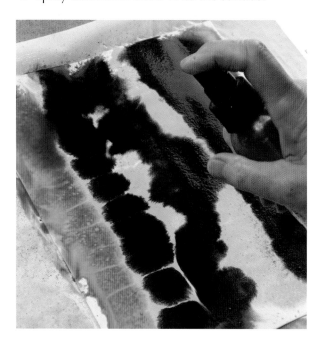

5. Use a sponge to pat the paint in selected areas until the entire surface is covered with color.

DYED SILK BACKGROUNDS

Dye-na-Flow works wonderfully for dyeing silk habotai. When using dyes, be sure to cover the work surface with plastic and wear protective gloves to prevent staining. Dyed silk can be given textural interest while the paint is still wet by sprinkling large-grained salt onto the wet fabric. I prefer Jacquard Silk Salt, but rock salt or other large-grained salt also works well. When dry, the salt is brushed off, revealing interesting patterns.

1. Lay the silk habotai on a work surface covered with plastic and inexpensive paper. You can also lay the silk on the paper side of freezer paper—the paper will absorb the dye through the silk and can be used later for collage. If you want to dye up to three pieces of silk at one time, layer the fabrics and spread them out as flat as possible. Spray each layer of silk with water using a spray bottle.

2. Apply Dye-na-Flow to the surface of the silk using Dye-na-Flow applicator bottles or an eyedropper.

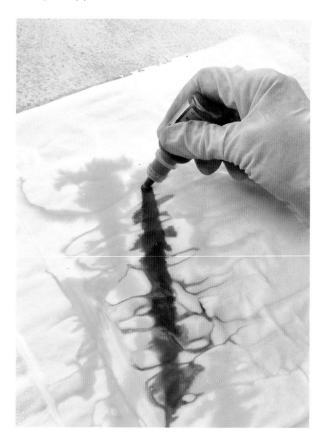

3. Repeat step two as necessary until you are satisfied with the result. If desired, use a sponge square to pat the color around so all areas of the fabric are covered with dye.

4. To create optional salt patterns, sprinkle salt over the surface while the dye is wet.

5. If you have salt on the top piece, leave all the pieces in place and let them dry. If you didn't use salt, but dyed more than one piece of silk, carefully separate the layers and lay them on deli paper, the shiny side of freezer paper, or plastic until dry.

6. After the silk is dry, if you have salt on the surface, brush the salt onto a piece of paper or plastic. Save the salt for use on a future project.

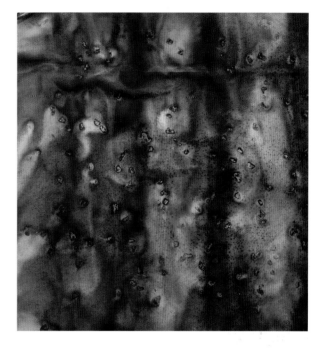

7. Cover your ironing board with a Teflon pressing sheet. To heat set the silk, iron the silk on the hottest setting of your iron. Make sure every part of the silk is heat set. Bring the ironed silk to a sink and wash out any residual dye with soap and water. Wring out the silk and iron it a second time on the hottest setting of your iron, placing it once again on a Teflon ironing sheet.

SPONGED BACKGROUNDS

1. If using a paper surface, lightly mist the back of the paper with water to prevent buckling (not necessary if working with fabric).

2. Apply paint to a palette and dip a wet or dry sponge into the paint. Or you can apply paint directly to the sponge, either by dipping the sponge into paint held in the jar lid or by squeezing applicator-tipped paint onto the sponge. Sponge the paint onto the design surface.

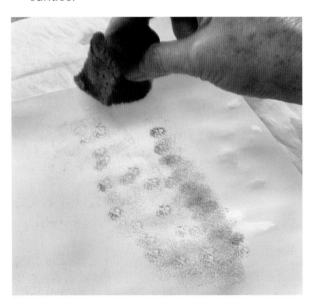

3. Sponge additional colors onto the design surface, overlapping layers and creating patterns if desired.

4. Repeat the process until you are satisfied with the results.

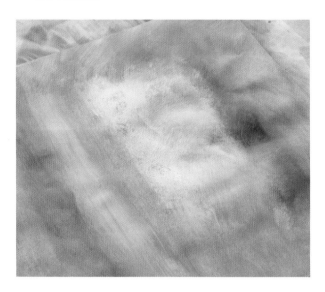

RUBBER-STAMPED BACKGROUNDS

1. Lightly mist the design surface with water, unless it has previously been painted. Apply paint to a sponge square and pat the color onto the rubber stamp.

2. Turn the rubber stamp face down onto the surface and press your fingers over the back of the rubber stamp. Then lift the stamp off the surface to reveal the image. It is possible to cover a large area of the design surface quickly if you use a very large rubber stamp.

3. Stamp additional images onto the surface using different rubber stamps and paint colors as desired.

4. Continue stamping images across the background until satisfied with the results.

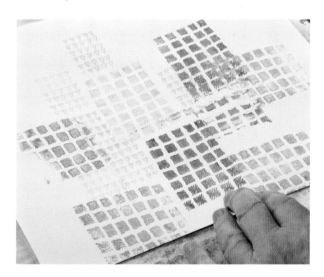

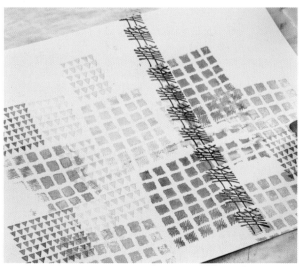

5. Wet a sponge with water. Apply transparent colors with a dry sponge to selected areas, or apply color over the stamped surface using a wet sponge to create a wash of color over the images.

6. Repeat step 5 with additional paint colors, overlapping colors as desired, until you are satisfied with the results.

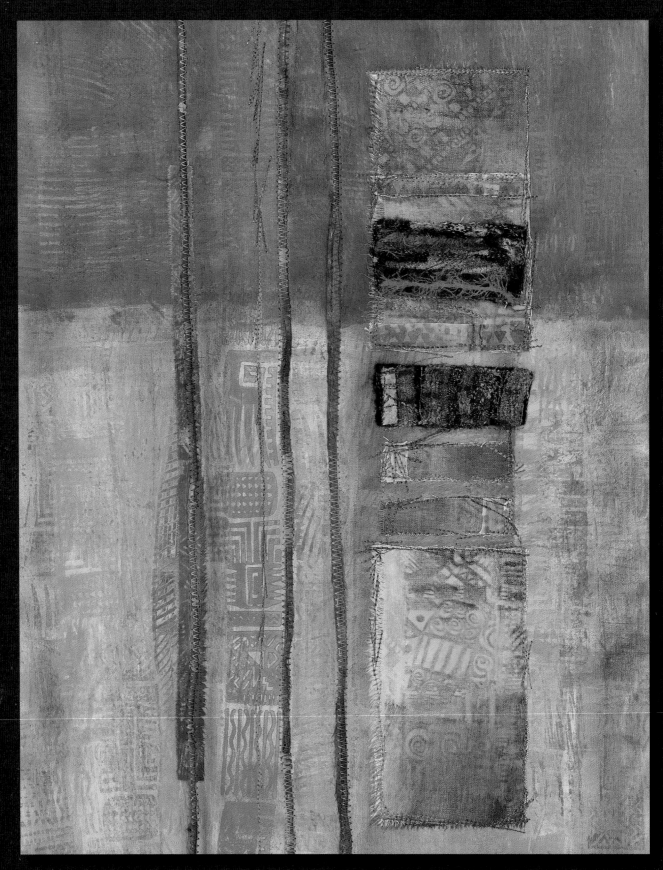

Size, balance, and repetition. Darker colors have more visual weight than lighter colors, so I balanced a large yellow area at bottom with a band of blue at top. To balance the row of wide, and mostly light-colored, rectangles at right, I added a narrow strip of dark blue at left. Throughout the piece I stitched blue, yellow, and orange thread for continuity.

DESIGN AND COMPOSITION IDEAS FOR ALL MEDIA— CREATING PIZZAZZ

After teaching for many years for stores, quilt guilds, painting groups, and schools, I've discovered that the one issue I consistently encounter is that students have problems with creating dynamic compositions. They create gorgeous painted and textured pieces to use in their creations, but then are at a loss when trying to put everything together to make a whole. This chapter will help you add pizzazz to your work. You are creating a symphony of lines, colors, values, and textures in your finished composition.

Pairing vertical and horizontal. The jagged yellow-and-gold vertical area in the middle brings a strong light to the center of the composition, while rows of horizontal purple rectangles on either side create movement.

COMPOSITION GUIDELINES

- **Balance** large shapes by repeating smaller shapes nearby.

- **Repeat** colors and/or shapes throughout a composition to maintain continuity.

- **Contrast elements,** such as colors, shapes, and lines.

- **Add texture** to make a composition visually exciting.

- **Use both vertical and horizontal elements** for movement and balance.

- **Add a focal point** by introducing a new color or by making one area brighter or darker than the rest.

- **Create movement.** Try not to place important, bold design elements near the top, bottom, or four corners of a composition. You don't want your eye to be interrupted from moving harmoniously through the design.

CREATING DYNAMIC COMPOSITIONS USING COLOR

Color is one of the most important components of a design. Color sets the mood for all creative pieces.

COMPLEMENTARY COLOR PALETTES

Complementary colors, or color-wheel opposites, tend to vibrate and create visual tension. To add more interest to a piece, use both darks and lights of the same colors.

Red and green. I used an intense red for this background, adding light areas of color with both vertical and horizontal gold shapes. Complementary bits of green appear throughout. The row of alternating light and dark vertical strips at bottom adds texture and balances the horizontal lines and rectangles above.

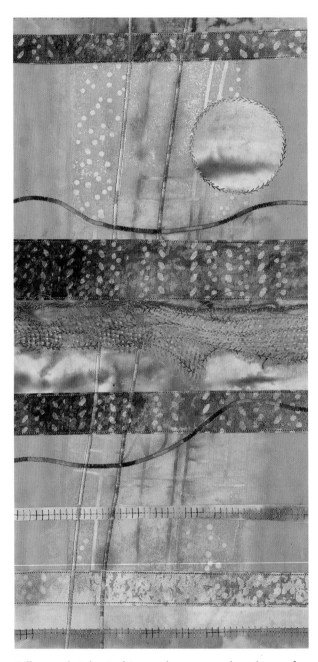

Yellow and violet. In this complementary color scheme of yellows and purples, I repeated horizontal bars from top to bottom. To add visual tension, I satin stitched two lines at a slight diagonal and two wavy lines on the horizontal. Using the same fabrics and papers throughout coordinates all the elements.

WARM AND COOL COLOR PALETTES

Choosing a dominant color scheme and accenting it with colors outside the scheme makes your work more interesting. I like to use a predominantly warm palette and then mix in some cool areas or a dominantly cool palette highlighted by warm accents.

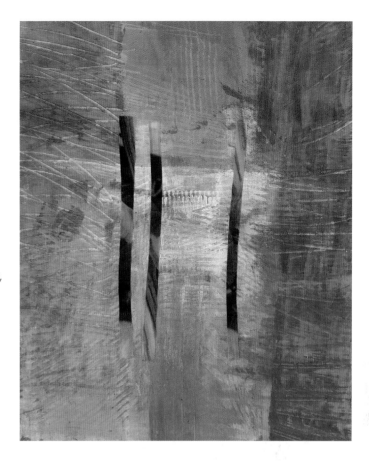

Predominantly cool colors. Cool darks at left and right give this piece its drama. In the middle, a long reddish orange shape changes to reddish violet, creating an interesting warm area in the middle.

Predominantly warm colors. This piece is predominantly orange and red. To make the composition more interesting, I placed a variety of cool shapes at the top, bottom, and sides. Vertical elements break up the huge orange-and-red space in the middle. On the longest vertical strip, I stitched three buttons to create a focal point.

EARTHTONE AND BRIGHT COLOR PALETTES

It's fun to mix a variety of colors in your work. I use earth colors with more vibrant colors to create interesting compositions.

Predominantly earth colors. This design works because color moves throughout. While the background is predominantly warm orange and gold, there are also cool blue shapes near the bottom. In the three dark, visually heavy rectangles, orange lines accent various shapes to incorporate the warm background color and prevent the dark rectangles from becoming too dominant. Two metallic gold lines provide focal interest.

CREATING DYNAMIC COMPOSITIONS USING REPETITION

Repetition is a key design principle to consider when producing creative work. It helps add continuity to a composition. Repetition can involve repeating shapes, colors, lines, or other elements.

Repetition of line. Here, I repeated vertical shapes and rectangles to create a dynamic composition. The background is very busy. To make all the elements work together, I added the three strong orange vertical lines over rust-colored rectangles. To balance the orange lines, I added a long blue-and-green vertical shape at left and three small rectangles at right. To repeat the strong orange, I stitched heavy reddish orange lines across the long blue vertical shape. A single horizontal line of gold paint, applied with an applicator tip, connects all the vertical elements.

Repetition of color. I painted this design on cardstock and unified the composition by repeating the aqua-and-lilac color scheme at left, right, and top. Vibrant orange acts as a focal point and complements the various shades of purple.

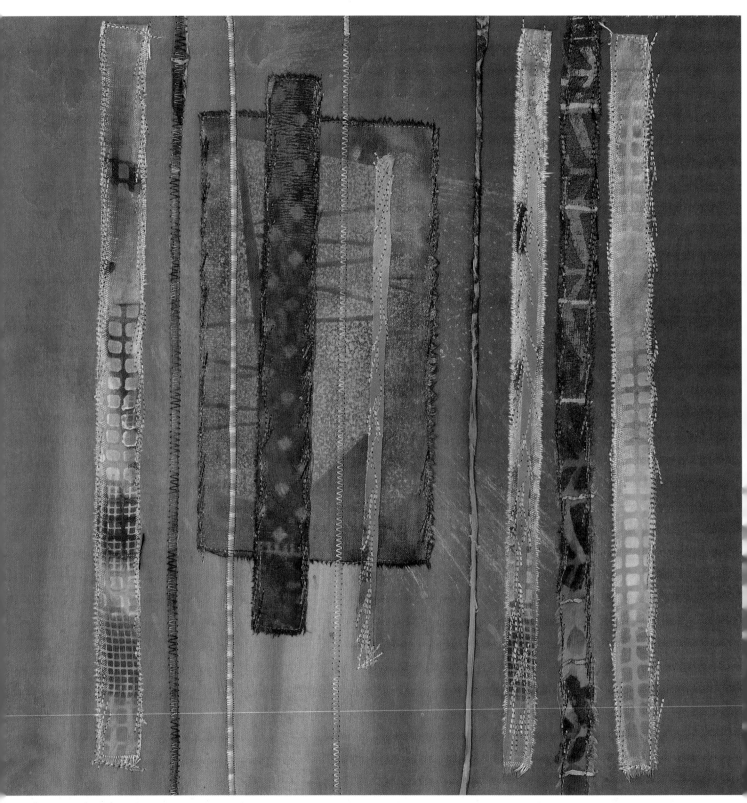

Repetition of line. Repeating vertical lines of different widths and lengths draws interest. Some lines are satin stitches produced with a sewing machine and others are appliquéd fabric. One is a piece of twisted fabric cord. Notice how the subtle color striping on the painted cotton background echoes the dominant lines on the surface.

CREATING DYNAMIC COMPOSITIONS USING PAINTING TECHNIQUES

Color washes, applicator-tipped lines, glazing with transparent colors, and metallic colors can all add pizzazz to a composition.

USING APPLICATOR-TIPPED PAINT

I use paint in squeeze bottles with a metal applicator tip attached to highlight areas of my composition with lines, dots, and patterns. I use colors that coordinate with or enhance the original design. I start with Jacquard squeeze bottles and then add a metal applicator to the end of the bottle. Always test the bottle before applying the paint, because the tip can become clogged. Use a straight pin on the applicator tip to remove dry paint. Dye-na-Flow is the only Jacquard squeeze bottle unable to receive an applicator tip. However, by gently squeezing the Dye-na-Flow bottle, you can still apply lines of paint as well as dots, dashes, wavy lines, or any other linear design.

Applicator-tipped lines. This composition is a very busy one. To make it work, I repeated a series of vertical shapes across the design. I made a large rubber-stamped rectangle at right. I softened the rectangle by appliquéing a piece of ExtravOrganza over the middle of it. To bring light to a very dark design, I highlighted vertical shapes along the edges with applicator-tipped lines of gold paint. To finish, I appliquéd a piece of fabric cord and added a strong red line right of center.

USING METALLIC OR PEARLESCENT COLORS

I use various metallic colors in many of my compositions. I like the reflective quality of metallic paint, and it often adds excitement to the design.

Metallic paint. Scrapbook paper printed with a digital image was the base for this design. After glazing over the design with color washes to soften the background, I rubber stamped a vertical series of metallic gold images to the left of center. To add some darks, I painted the violet vertical dashed line, and the two violet vertical lines, with a flat brush.

USING COLOR WASHES

Sometimes I create a design that has too many conflicting colors. I've learned that I can solve this design problem by washing a color over the entire design to make the elements work together.

Color washes. A black-and-white design on illustration board was the starting point for this composition. I painted blocks of colors over the black-and-white design. Then I layered washes of bronze over the color layers, letting some of the bright colors show through. I also added vertical stripes of violet just to the left of center.

CREATING DYNAMIC COMPOSITIONS USING CONTRAST

In a composition, contrast comes in many forms. It can be a subtle (or bold) color change. It can be variations in texture or value. It can come from using different techniques next to one another.

Contrast in colors. Here, a mostly cool composition features contrasting warm areas. I painted, rubber stamped, and sponged layers of colors onto a fabric background. Then I added several pieces of fabric appliqué. In addition, I sewed a piece of fabric cord and several vertical lines of zigzag stitching to the background. To finish the piece, I used applicator-tipped paint to highlight selected areas.

Contrast in textures. While the background is a piece of painted fabric, inkjet ExtravOrganza pieces, decorative stitching, and painted paper and fabric appliqués create a variety of textures. Highlighting areas with colored pencil adds still more visual dimension.

Contrast in values. Light vertical strips shimmer amid dark purples and muted layers of color. I started with a heavy piece of Bristol board, and then made Styrofoam prints across the background. I collaged layers of paper to the surface, letting some of the Styrofoam-print areas show through. You can see the prints on the right and in between some of the stripes. A button and three air-dry clay embellishments add dimension. Highlights applied with applicator-tipped paint complete the piece.

CREATING DYNAMIC COMPOSITIONS USING TEXTURE

I like to use a variety of materials within a single piece to create texturally interesting designs. The finished composition becomes much more intricate and appealing. Try different media and embellishments within one composition. You can add rubber-stamped areas, paint, ribbons, metal brads, textural pieces of paper, painted fabric, threads, digital images, and any other media or embellishments desired.

Varied texture. Heavy cardstock was stamped and painted to create a background. Several collage elements, including painted paper, three narrow yellow wooden sticks, five vertical blue ribbons, and a cluster of tiny gold beads were glued to the surface. Combining a variety of elements and techniques creates both actual and visual texture.

A line of fabric cord floats above a complex mixture of colors and textures, creating a focal point.

CREATING FABRIC CORD

I wanted to create a flexible fabric cord that would be easy to appliqué or glue onto projects. I experimented with different techniques and ultimately ended up with two types of cord. One cord is created by tearing the dyed, rolled edge from a silk scarf. I created the second type of cord by twisting narrow strips of wet painted fabric and heat setting them to retain their shape.

CREATING TWISTED CORD

1. Tear or cut a piece of painted fabric into strips about ⅜" wide. If the strip is narrower, it will be a thin fabric cord. If the strip is wider, it will be a thicker fabric cord.

2. Wet the fabric by dipping it in water or by spraying it with water.

3. On an ironing board, twist the end of the fabric tightly and hold it in place with the tip of the iron. Continue twisting a little of the strip at a time and iron along the length to set the shape. Work your way from one end of the strip to the other, twisting and ironing until the cord is completely dry.

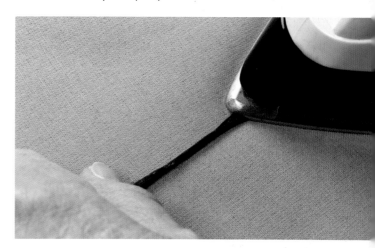

4. Repeat steps 1–3 with additional strips of painted fabric to make the desired number of cords.

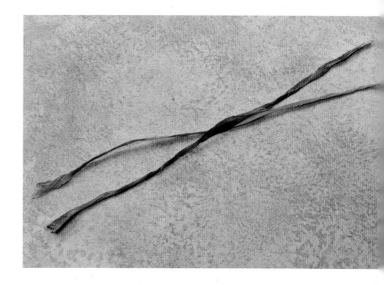

For each of the compositions above and at right, I stitched torn pieces of painted delicatessen paper together by hand to create a background. I hand stitched more deli paper to the background for contrast and to create focal areas.

DELICATESSEN PAPER COLLAGE

I've been hooked on using delicatessen paper ever since a friend showed it to me years ago. I put it under all of my work when I'm painting. If I'm painting fabric, the paint seeps through the fabric to the delicatessen paper below. I end up with stacks of marvelous paper covered with incredible designs. I intended to create collages with the paper I've been saving, and I've finally done it in this chapter. The paper comes in 12" x 12" and 14" x 14" sheets in boxes of 1000 sheets and is available in different weights. The paper is water resistant (not waterproof) and even when wet, the paper doesn't buckle. The paper is heavy enough to take quite a beating. It can be ironed, wrinkled, torn, cut, and otherwise manipulated. I can add more paint, colored pencil, dye, crayon, or any other water-based or dry media to it. The paper can be sewn easily to fabric projects because it is so sturdy. Pre-folded delicatessen paper sheets are not as sturdy, so really look at the paper before you buy it.

CREATING COLLAGES WITH PAINTED DELICATESSEN PAPER

1. Select a large piece of previously painted or rubber-stamped delicatessen paper to use as the background for the collage. Tear additional pieces of deli paper into collage elements. Use a glue stick or white glue to attach the collage elements to the background paper.

2. Glue additional deli-paper collage elements to the background paper.

3. Hand or machine stitch along the edges of the deli-paper collage elements where they overlap the background paper. If hand stitching, use a double layer of thread for more impact. Leave some elements unstitched, if desired.

These pieces were assembled from bits of deli paper that had been either hand or machine stitched together. Some were also painted after the collage elements had been attached to the background. The composition shown at lower right, opposite, is embellished with two air-dry clay pieces and two lengths of fabric cord.

4. Add more paint and other collage elements to the composition if desired to complete the design.

GALLERY

The "stitched" background for this piece is actually a printed image on cardstock. The stamped turtle design in the middle is a piece of inkjet-printed fabric. I glued strips of a different inkjet-printed fabric at the right and left of the turtle. Using an embossing folder with uneven parallel lines, I created two abstract Cuttlebug textures from digital prints and then glued them to the top and bottom of the middle section. To complete the piece, I used a fine-line brown permanent marker to accent selected areas.

PROVO CRAFT'S CUTTLEBUG

I was teaching at Stamping Details in Poway, California, when I was introduced to a marvelous machine called a Cuttlebug. It was love at first sight. I could immediately see the possibilities of creating textured painted pieces to use in my collage work. Since then, I've met the wonderful people at Provo Craft and they provided the embossing folders and dies used for this chapter. Provo Craft manufactures dozens of plastic embossing folders to create textured paper and many metal dies for cutting shapes with the Cuttlebug.

Thank you, Provo Craft, for your kindness and generosity.

CREATING TEXTURED PAPER WITH CUTTLEBUG EMBOSSING FOLDERS

1. Set up the Cuttlebug according the manufacturer's instructions.

2. Choose a piece of plain cardstock, painted paper, copy paper, or an inkjet print on cardstock or photo paper. Place an embossing folder over the paper and use as a guide to mark the width to cut the paper.

3. Cut the paper so that it's slightly smaller than the marked width of the plastic embossing folder. Place the trimmed paper into the embossing folder.

4. Place the embossing folder between the plastic cutting pads and onto the spacer, following the manufacturer's instructions. The folded edge of the folder should be next to the roller used to advance the pieces through the machine.

5. Roll the embossing folder through the Cuttlebug's rollers to create a piece of textured paper. There should be enough pressure on the paper within the sleeve to make an impression. The Cuttlebug comes with plastic pads in various thicknesses and it might take experimentation to find the right combination of plastic pads to make the impression you want.

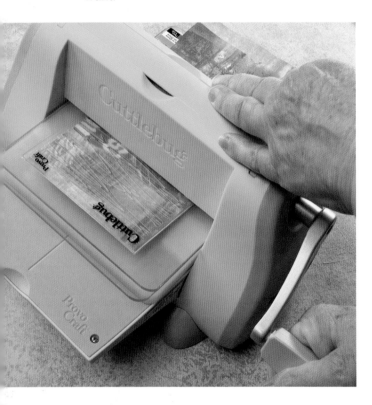

6. Leave the paper as it is or select another embossing folder and run the same piece of paper through the Cuttlebug a second time, creating a more complex design.

7. Leave the textured piece as is, or use a flat brush with paint to highlight selected textured areas. Remove most of the paint from the brush, creating a dry brush. Paint the raised textures of the design with the dry brush to highlight them. Paint additional layers of color as needed.

CREATING DIE-CUT DESIGNS USING THE CUTTLEBUG

The Cuttlebug dies come in wonderful shapes and alphabets. The Cuttlebug, when used with a die, cuts paper into shapes or letters to use in your creative designs. The great part about using the Cuttlebug with the dies is that you create both positive and negative shapes to use in your creative work.

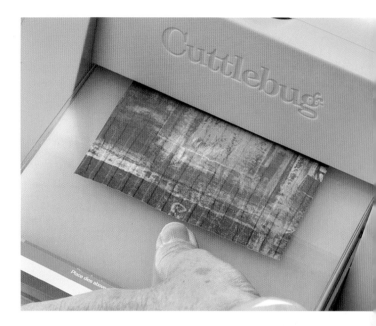

1. Set up the Cuttlebug following the manufacturer's instructions. Place the die, foam side up, on a Cuttlebug cutting pad. If you accidentally have the metal side up, you can bend the metal, so always place the foam side up. Cut a piece of plain, painted, or inkjet-printed cardstock (not copy paper) slightly smaller than the width of the Cuttlebug cutting pads.

2. Lay the cardstock on top of the die and place the plastic cutting pad on the bed of the Cuttlebug. Roll the pieces through the Cuttlebug.

3. Remove the cardstock from the cutting pads and punch out the designs. Remember to keep all of the pieces to use in your projects. To save time, create several die-cuts at one time and store them for future use.

GALLERY

An inkject print on cardstock was the starting point for this design. I added inkjet-printed fabric and several textured Cuttlebug pieces to the background and accented areas with permanent fine-line black and brown markers.

I used the Cuttlebug twice here. First, I made an alphabet piece from inkjet-printed cardstock. I punched out the letters and set them aside for other projects; then I attached the negative piece to the right side of the design and painted around the punched-out letters. The letters in the middle of the design were painted using a brass stencil. I used the Cuttlebug again to make small frame-shaped pieces that I glued to the background and painted. The background for this piece is painted and rubber-stamped cardstock.

This piece demonstrates the wonderful versatility of the Cuttlebug. I began with an inkjet-printed cardstock background enhanced by layers of paint and some rubber stamping, and then added two Cuttlebug strips for texture. The first piece, to the left of center, has swirly designs and layers of paint with metallic highlights. The second piece is the lilac dot pattern that runs down the middle of the design. Using the Cuttlebug a third time, I added part of an alphabet. Three painted fabric pieces, two cardstock pieces, and some painted metallic highlights finish the collage.

I used a leaf-patterned piece of inkjet-printed cardstock for the background and painted layers of color over it. Then I painted inkjet pieces, tore them into strips, and glued them to the surface in four places. I used the Cuttlebug to make the small frame on the left as well as the waffle-like die-cut square on the right, which repeats the other square shape. Dark brown ultra-fine-line marker outlines selected areas.

This melted crayon piece began with a digital image printed onto photographic paper with an inkjet printer. Layers of melted crayon were added, but because the paper was shiny, each new layer of crayon removed some of the previous layer, revealing the inkjet image below.

CRAYONS AND OIL PASTELS

We all love crayons. I can remember as a child coming home from the store with a brand new box of crayons and a coloring book. I could lay on the floor, face down, involved in coloring for hours. I still love crayons and go to every possible dollar or 99-cent store to buy more. In this chapter you will learn how to do rubbings with crayons and oil pastels to make designs with visual texture. You'll be amazed by the results produced when creating melted-crayon designs. The melted-crayon process is wonderful when used with digital images printed on shiny paper. The shiny paper resists crayon build up, allowing new layers to remove color from the previous layers. This permits the inkjet design below to reveal itself. I hope to share some crayon and oil pastel ideas that you haven't tried before.

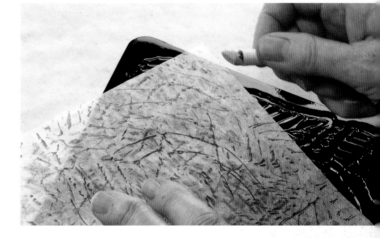

CRAYON RUBBINGS ON DELI PAPER

1. Place a rubbing plate or any flat textured item on top of the work surface and place a piece of very thin deli paper or fabric on top. Use the side of a crayon to rub over the paper or fabric to create a pattern. Move the paper or fabric and repeat until satisfied with the results.

2. Remove the rubbing plate. Sponge Jacquard Textile Traditionals in different colors, lighter colors first, over the rubbings. The rubbings will show through the transparent paint.

3. When the paint is dry, tear the deli paper or cut or tear the fabric into smaller pieces to use in your creative work.

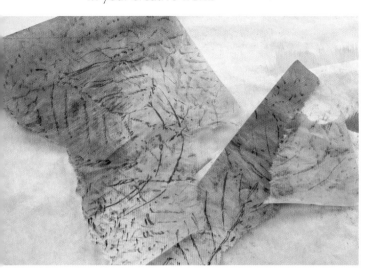

OIL PASTEL RUBBINGS ON DELI PAPER OR FABRIC

1. Place a rubbing plate or any flat textured item on top of the work surface and lay a piece of very thin deli paper or white, colored, or previously painted fabric on top of the plate (printed muslin was used in this sample). The higher the thread count of the fabric, the better the impressions will be. Use the side of an oil pastel to apply color to the design surface. Continue with additional colors to create a pattern.

2. Move the paper or fabric on the rubbing plate as necessary to create a pattern over the entire piece. Continue until satisfied with the results.

3. Remove the rubbing plate. Sponge Jacquard Textile Traditionals, lighter colors first, over the rubbings. The rubbings will show through the paint.

4. If you did the rubbings on fabric, place the finished design between layers of copy paper, and then between two Teflon sheets. Heat set the color using the hottest setting of a dry iron.

MELTED CRAYONS

A dear friend of mine, Joan Vaupen, gave a lesson to my experimental painting group, and part of the lesson involved using crayons on paper on a warming tray. I had done this technique before, but I got so excited by the possibilities that I was obsessed with this technique for weeks. I like the idea that some of the pieces look like encaustic painting without all of the expensive equipment involved with encaustic painting.

BE CAREFUL

This technique is done with an electric griddle and is not for children. They could easily burn themselves. Do not heat the griddle so hot that it smokes. You want it just hot enough to melt the crayons without smoking.

1. Cover the surface of an electric griddle with extra heavy aluminum foil, and then plug it in and heat to about 275°.

2. Lay a piece of photographic paper (matte or shiny), a piece of white cardstock, a sheet of inkjet labels, a piece of white copy paper, or a digital image face up on the foil-covered heated griddle.

3. Hold the paper in place with a wooden spatula. Apply layers of crayon to the paper. As you add more crayon, some of the color below will blend with the new color or the new color will remove the first color applied. Since all griddles vary, watch for smoking and turn down the temperature if smoke appears. If the crayons aren't melting well, turn the griddle temperature up slightly.

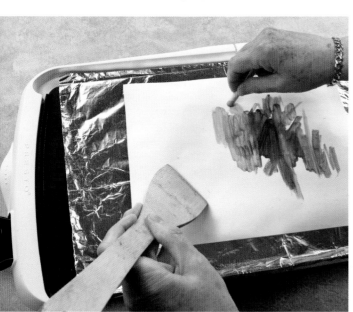

4. If desired, use an old brush to move the color on the paper. The crayon won't come out of the brush, but the brush can be used over and over on future crayon-melting designs. Wipe the brush on a paper towel to clean it, or brush it on the hot foil-covered griddle and wipe it on a paper towel. Repeat as needed.

5. Use a white candle (not paraffin, which will smoke and burn) if desired to move the crayon colors around and add some transparency.

6. Buff the crayon layers with a tissue to remove any excess crayon bits from the surface.

7. To heat set the finished piece, place it between two sheets of deli paper. Place the deli paper and artwork between Teflon pressing sheets. Press with an iron on the highest setting. Some crayon and oil pastel colors will transfer onto the deli paper. The deli paper can be used later for collage.

GALLERY

 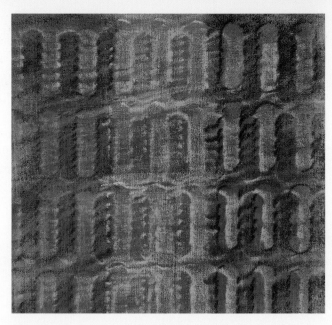

These rubbings started as fabric painted with Dye-na-Flow. I placed a rubber kitchen mat under the fabric and made long oval shapes with metallic light blue oil pastel. For more texture, I placed another rubber shower mat under the piece on the left, and then added violet and metallic gold lines. I used the same colors to highlight the middle of the piece on the right.

A variety of rubbings on deli paper shows a range of patterns and colors.

I used different colors of oil pastels and a commercial rubbing plate to make rubbings on white fabric. I then sponged several layers of Jacquard Textile Traditionals over the surface, leaving a bright yellow area.

An unsuccessful piece of painted fabric in magenta, turquoise, and violet was salvaged by texturing with lilac and gold oil pastels. I rubbed on both sides of kitchen and shower mats to create layers of color, letting some of the background show through, especially the turquoise area on the right.

To achieve a painterly effect on this melted-crayon piece, I used a white candle to thin the colors and to move the color around on the surface of the heavy cardstock. I applied candle and crayon to a sheet of inkjet address labels and pressed two of the labels to the crayon surface. One label is shown in the detail photo at right; the second label was cut in half lengthwise and placed to the left of the design's center.

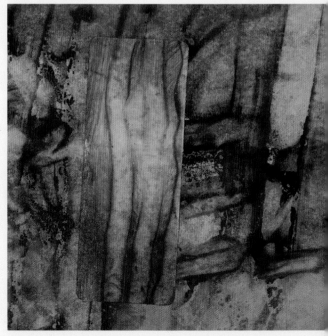

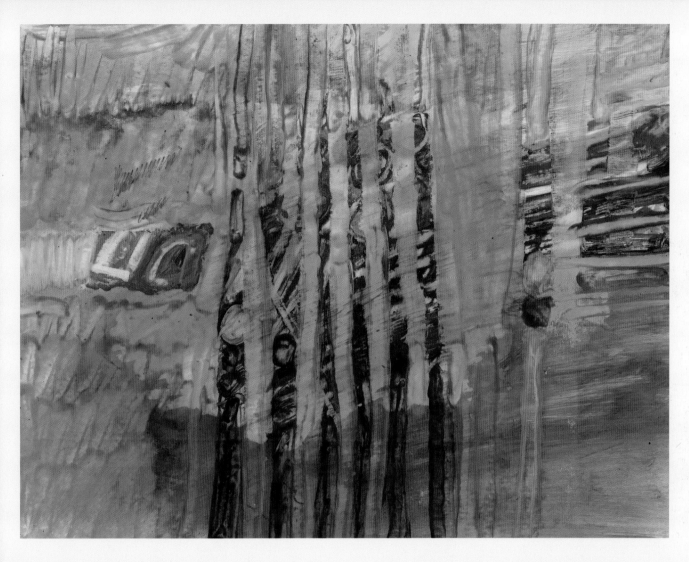

These designs were created on white cardstock. I simply applied layers of crayon and white candle wax to the surface and built up colors until I was satisfied. The photo below is a detail of the piece at right.

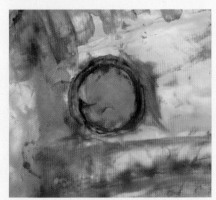

I created this composition in color design with a computer program. I printed it in black and white, and then added color back with colored pencils.

COLORED PENCILS

When I taught high school art, teaching colored-pencil techniques was paramount in my curriculum. The students loved the possibilities. The ease of using colored pencils and the fact they you can add additional colors and values easily to any project make them a great choice for your creative endeavors. I use them on paper, fabric, inkjet images, Cuttlebug pieces, wet-into-wet pieces and just about any other place where they will adhere. After doing your collage, appliqué, painting, sponging, resist, or other technique, use colored pencils to highlight areas or to add lines, textures, dots, crosshatching, or solid areas of color to the piece.

Exercise 2. Do the reverse of exercise 1. Color an area with red, and then color over a portion of it with yellow.

Exercise 3. Color an area with yellow, and then color over a portion of it with blue.

COLORED-PENCIL LAYERING EXERCISE

Layer the colors using medium pressure. If you press too hard on the lead, it will be difficult to add additional colors. The result will be different depending upon which color is on the top and bottom. The key to making gorgeous colored pencil work is to layer from the lightest colors to the darkest colors. It is difficult to color over dark areas once you have applied the color.

Exercise 1. Color an area with yellow, and then color over a portion of it with red.

Exercise 4. Do the reverse of exercise 3. Color an area with blue, and then color over a portion of it with yellow.

Exercise 5. Color an area with red, and then color over a portion of it with blue.

Exercise 6. Do the reverse of exercise 5. Color an area with blue, and then color over a portion of it with red.

Exercise 7. Layer other colors and see what happens. Think of the colored pencils as looking through stained glass windows. As you apply each layer, the color below will show through.

COLORED PENCILS OVER DIGITAL IMAGES

Using colored pencil over digital images is a snap. You can print an image as it is or lighten it so that it's easier to color. I use Picasa 3 because of its ease of use and easy printing technology. It is a free program from Google. To download it into your computer, type Picasa into your internet browser and follow the downloading instructions. Spend some time reviewing the features.

If you have a color printer that allows you to continue printing when some ink colors have run out, you can continue to use the ink cartridge to print irregularly colored images that can be enhanced with colored pencils.

1. Start with a digital image printed onto paper. Begin by layering colored pencil over the digital image. Color in entire areas or add color or lines to highlight areas of the image.

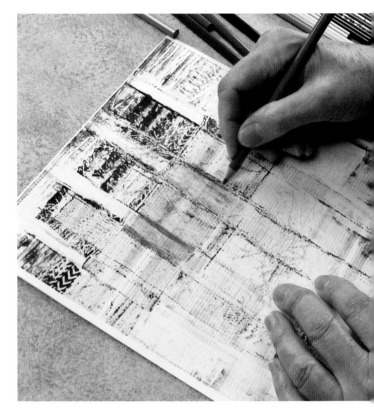

2. Keep building layers of color from light to dark, using a light hand, until you are happy with the result.

Here, photo-editing software was used to alter a digital photo of a leaf by erasing some of the background and intensifying the color. After printing the photo, I layered colored pencil over the leaf and background.

Although it's placed here in the colored-pencil chapter, this piece incorporates several techniques. First, I created the background by printing a digital image of one of my art pieces onto fabric. Then I appliquéd six pieces of fabric to the surface using a narrow machine buttonhole stitch. I ended by applying layers of color and lines to the surface with colored pencil.

The middle of this piece was created by sewing two layers of fabric together and then cutting away parts of the top layer to reveal the layer below (detail at left). I stitched fabrics colored with melted crayon to the each side of the middle piece, then added layers of colored pencil to all three sections of the assembled unit. Two appliquéd strips of rubber-stamped fabric and a fabric cord, along with several lines of buttonhole stitching in various widths, add texture to the assemblage.

The free-flowing and abstract shapes in the background were made using a wet-into-wet technique on fabric. Colored pencils were used to isolate some of the shapes. The piece is embellished with layers of thread topped by a piece of textured yarn. Straight stitching outlines some of the free-form shapes.

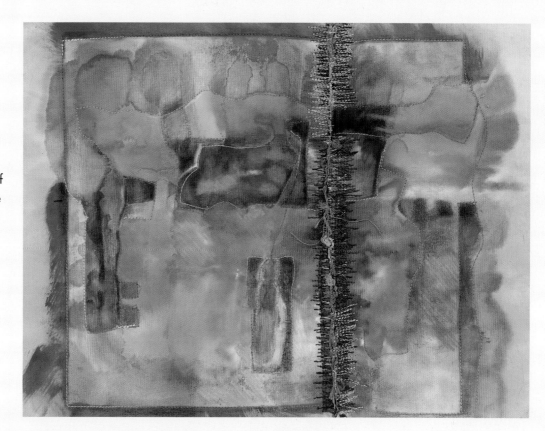

Shapes cut from masking tape acted as a resist when I painted and rubber stamped the background. When I finished painting, I removed the tape and added layers of colored pencil to highlight and deepen selected areas with color. To finish the piece, I sewed narrow lines of buttonhole stitch around the resist shapes.

I used a brayer over several different textured rubbing plates and then applied many different paint colors. Then I brayered a piece of fabric, tore it into three strips, and appliquéd them to the background.

BRAYER TECHNIQUES

Using a brayer is such fun and produces amazing work. Painting with a brayer produces interesting pieces that can be used for backgrounds. Using a brayer and paint in combination with rubbing plates produces patterns with visual texture. I used Jacquard's Lumiere, Textile Traditionals, and Neopaque for this technique.

CREATING PATTERNS WITH A BRAYER AND PAINT

1. Apply paint to a freezer-paper palette. You can apply more than one color of paint to the palette if desired.

2. Roll the brayer in the paint, and then roll the brayer over the chosen surface. On smooth paper you will get one effect; on fabric you will get another effect. Experiment with different surfaces.

3. Repeat the process with additional paint colors until satisfied with the results.

4. Apply a contrasting paint to the palette and roll the brayer through it. Then roll the brayer across a rubbing plate or other texture, such as a kitchen-sink mat to create a pattern on the brayer.

5. Roll the brayer across the design surface to transfer the pattern on the brayer to the design surface.

7. Continue adding brayered designs, prints, or additional paint with the brayer until satisfied with the results.

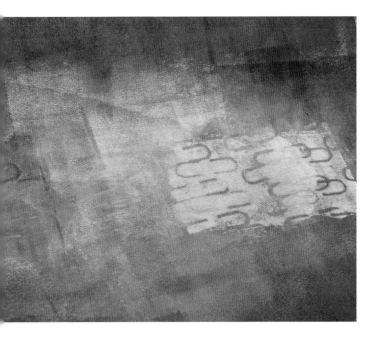

6. Continue to add brayered patterns to the design surface as desired. To make a textural print, apply paint to a flat textural item, such as a kitchen-sink mat, and then turn the mat over and press it onto the design surface.

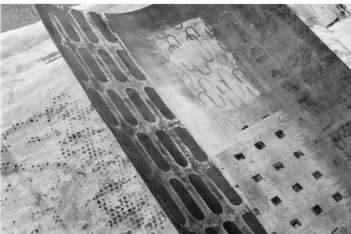

CREATING PATTERNED FABRIC WITH RUBBING PLATES AND A BRAYER

This is an unbelievably easy process and can be done over plain, colored, or previously painted fabric pieces. The paint needs to be thick, rather than thin. I like to use Jacquard Neopaque, Textile Traditionals, and Lumiere. It is possible to create layers and layers of visual texture with this process.

1. Apply paint to a palette. You can apply more than one color of paint to the palette and mix with a palette knife if desired.

2. Place a rubbing plate or other textured surface, such as a kitchen-sink mat, under a piece of fabric.

3. Roll the brayer in the paint. Roll the brayer over the fabric, revealing the texture below.

5. Continue as in step 4 until satisfied with the results.

4. Reposition the fabric on the rubbing plate or textured surface, or change to a different textured surface if desired. Add more paint to the palette or use a new palette for a new color of paint, if desired. Apply additional paint colors to the fabric using the brayer.

GALLERY

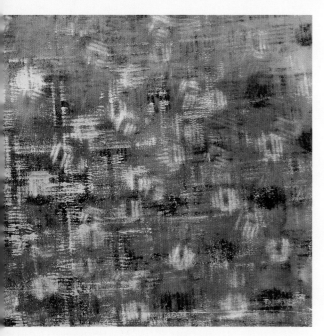

This piece of plain cotton fabric was transformed when a brayer was used to apply a variety of paint colors over a textured rubbing mat.

The base for this design was a piece of fabric printed using the gelatin technique (see page 101). I placed a shower mat, wrong side up, under the fabric and applied paint to it with a brayer, resulting in the polka-dot pattern.

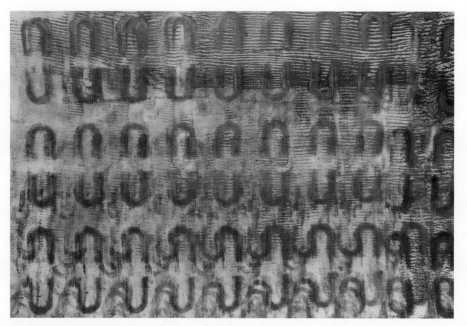

Here, a painted and stamped piece of polyester fabric was given depth with the help of a textured kitchen mat. The mat was placed under the fabric, and then contrasting paint was applied to the fabric using a brayer. Both the U-shaped pattern and the narrow red lines were created by rolling a paint-loaded brayer across the fabric.

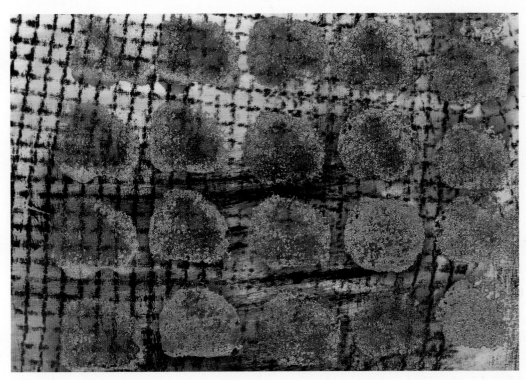

The grid pattern was created by placing painted cotton fabric sponged with a variety of paints over a heavy rug-hooking canvas and applying black paint with a brayer. Metallic shapes were then sponged across the surface.

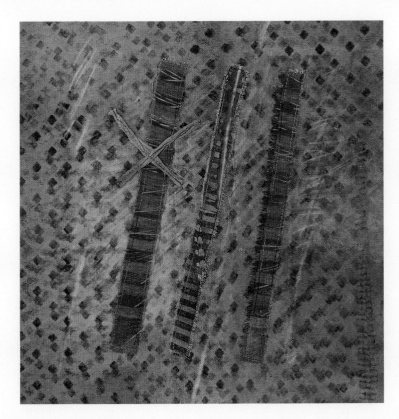

This highly patterned design is the result of placing a rubbing plate under the fabric and using the brayer to apply several layers of paint to it. Painted fabric strips and pieces of fabric cord were stitched on by machine.

Dyed cosmetic pads, near the top right corner, are stitched to the background with variegated thread and topped with fabric cord. More cosmetic pads, torn into free-form shapes, form a vertical column just to the left of center. Random stitching with variegated thread holds them in place.

COSMETIC COTTON PADS

I'm always asking myself "What if?" I'm always looking at ordinary items for possibilities to use them in different ways. While teaching a class in Oregon, I decided to dye some ordinary cotton cosmetic pads with liquid paint and dye. While the pieces were wet, I found that I could separate them into two or three layers. One small package of cotton pads could yield hundreds of small embellishment pieces. The embellishments can be left as is for a soft feel or they can be sealed with matte or gloss medium to make them stiff. In addition, the dyed cotton pieces can be further embellished by gluing on threads and yarn to make even more interesting pieces. I discovered that the pads come in all shapes and sizes and that opened up other opportunities to be creative. The key word here is experiment. I use Jacquard Dye-na-Flow for dyeing cosmetic pads. When using dyes, be sure to cover the work surface with plastic and wear protective gloves to prevent staining.

PAINTED COSMETIC-COTTON-PAD EMBELLISHMENTS

1. Lay delicatessen paper on a plastic-covered work surface. Put on vinyl or other protective gloves. Dip cosmetic pads in a container of water and wring them out. Lay the cosmetic pads on top of the deli paper.

2. Apply Dye-na-Flow to the cotton pads with an applicator bottle or an eye dropper.

3. Squeeze the pads together to distribute the dye.

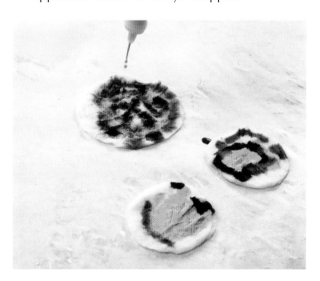

4. While the pads are wet, gently pull each one apart into two or three layers.

5. Lay the pads on the *dull* side of freezer paper or onto delicatessen paper to dry. If desired, apply matte or gloss medium to the pads to make them stiff after they are dry. To apply medium, place the cosmetic pads on the *shiny* side of the freezer paper so they can be removed easily after drying. Use the dull side of the freezer paper for wet items; they'll leave beautiful dyed patterns that can be used for collage work later.

6. Layer yarn over the cosmetic pad and brush with more matte or gloss medium. Let the embellishment dry.

7. Use the cosmetic cotton pad embellishment in your creative work. It is shown here over a painted background to create a focal point.

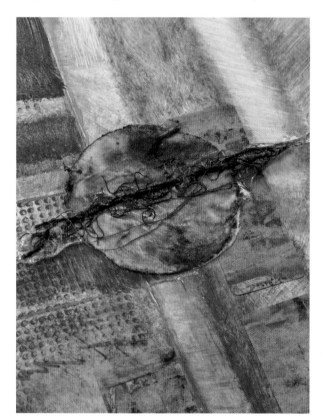

GALLERY

A single cotton cosmetic pad accents this vivid fabric piece. The background is a digital image printed onto fabric using an inkjet printer and nonpermanent inks. When the print was fresh out of the printer, I sprayed it with water to make the colors bleed. I then added paint and colored pencil and sewed narrow lines with a machine buttonhole stitch. The final touch is the cotton pad, which was glazed with matte medium and had yarns and threads glued to it.

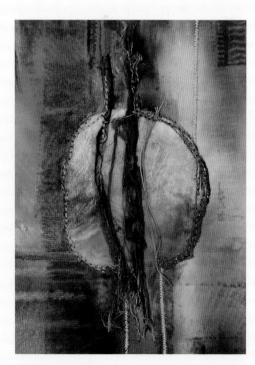

GALLERY

This collage is composed of delicatessen paper that was originally used to cover my work surface while I dyed cosmetic cotton pads. The dye spread from the cotton pads onto the deli paper. After the cotton pads dried, I removed them and set them aside, revealing circular patterns on the dyed deli paper. I tore pieces from the deli paper and stitched them together by machine. To balance the violets at the bottom, I appliquéd violet pieces of dyed cosmetic cotton pads at the upper-left corner of the piece.

This composition is made up of three pieces of painted fabric torn from different parts of one larger piece and then sewn back together. Torn strips of cotton pads were stitched to the surface in a vertical column near the center. Appliquéd bits of fabric—the long orange strip and the striped squares—add linear interest and unify the piece.

This piece is all about fiber in various forms. The background is painted fabric. Five painted violet fabric strips are appliquéd vertically to the background, with two dyed facial-wipe pieces sewn over them for contrast. The facial-wipe pieces are accented with textured yarns, and a fabric cord is stitched to the background between the pieces. A final and important addition is the two lines of machine stitching in brightly colored variegated thread.

FACIAL WIPES

After using some Oil of Olay facial wipes, I noticed that the surface of the wipes was very intriguing. The wipes for dry-to-normal skin were completely different than the ones for combination-to-oily skin types. I decided to try dyeing the wipes with Dye-na-Flow and see how they could be used in my creative work. Each wipe is about 4" x 6". I found that after heat setting the entire wipe, I could tear it and create gorgeous torn edges. The combination-to-oily wipe can also be separated into two pieces when hot from ironing, which produces a piece with holes and a piece with a diamond pattern. After discovering the magic of facial wipes, I bought every imaginable brand to test; all dyed beautifully and could be torn if I cut a slit into the edge.

Before dyeing the wipes, rinse them thoroughly to remove the cleansing agents. Let the wipes dry and store them for later use or dye them immediately. I usually use the wipes as they were intended, and then wash, rinse, and dry them, dyeing them at a later date. When using dyes, be sure to cover the work surface with plastic and wear protective gloves to prevent staining. After dyeing and heat setting, I store the wipes in plastic bags by color.

DYEING FACIAL WIPES

1. Dip a wipe into clean water, wring it out, and lay it on a plastic-covered work surface. Layer wipes to dye several at a time.

2. Apply Dye-na-Flow to the wipes, using an applicator-tipped bottle or an eyedropper. The color will start bleeding. Repeat with other colors as desired.

3. If you are dyeing several wipes, squeeze the wipes together and let the dye seep into the wipes.

4. Lay the wipes out to dry on deli paper or a piece of inexpensive white paper. The paper can be used for collage later.

5. After the wipes are dry, heat set them with a hot iron. If you have dyed an Oil of Olay combination-to-oily wipe, pull apart the two layers while the wipe is very hot to produce two pieces with different textures.

YARN AND THREAD FACIAL-WIPE EMBELLISHMENTS

1. Dilute matte medium with water using 75% medium and 25% water. If the mixture is too thin, the facial wipes will not adhere to each other. You may have to use the matte medium undiluted.

2. Tear the facial wipes into long pieces and overlap them on a piece of freezer paper. Apply matte medium liberally to the wipes to glue them together.

3. Lay threads, pieces of yarn, and any other bits of colored fiber over the wipes.

4. Apply matte medium liberally to the threads and the facial wipes. Use a tissue to carefully wipe away excess matte medium on the freezer paper. Let the piece dry completely overnight.

5. After the embellishment is dry, pull it off the freezer paper. You will notice dry matte medium around the edges where you could not remove it completely from the embellishment. Use tiny, sharp scissors to trim the excess matte medium, or leave it as is if it will be used in collage.

6. Use the facial-wipe embellishment in your creative work. It is shown here over a painted background to create a focal point.

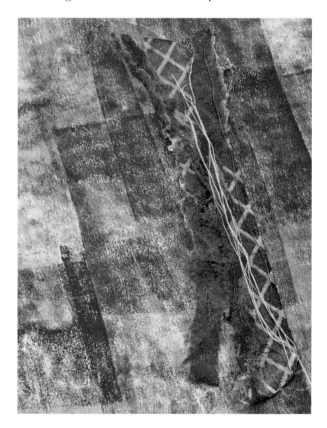

GALLERY

To make the collages above, I positioned torn strips of dyed facial wipes over a piece of dyed fabric, overlapping the edges, then stitched the strips to the background using straight stitches, zigzag stitches, and a variety of threads.

The pieces shown at left and below are painted cardstock, with additional rubber stamping and paint. Dyed pieces of facial wipes are glued to the surface and embellished with decorative threads.

This is one of my favorite pieces. I used a stiff place mat for the background, which accepted the layers of stitches and appliqué easily. The piece combines inkjet-printed cotton fabric and ExtravOrganza from Jacquard, as well as inkjet prints on paper. The surface is covered with straight and zigzag stitches. I sewed buttons and textured yarn to the design for dimension and included a variety of painted and molding-paste-textured fabrics on the right side. I created rubber-stamped patterns in selected areas using a variety of paints. The pictures are: my husband, Joel, and me in Mexico; my mother and father; and Joel on a pony when he was about four years old.

DIGITAL IMAGES

I have a complete fascination with the computer and its possibilities for the artist. With the ability to alter images with various programs designed for that purpose, the imagination is only limited by the individual's sense of play and curiosity. I take tons of photographs of everything, including textures, close-ups of every imaginable subject, my own artwork, family portraits, vacations, and everything in between. At this writing, I have about 40,000 images stored in an external hard drive plugged into my computer. I use Picasa 3 for sorting all of my images into folders. They are easy to access and the simple tools in Picasa make it easy to improve your images and create new ones. Check download.com for free digital image programs including Picasa 3. When using digital images in your creative work, be sure to respect copyright laws. Use photos you have taken yourself or use artwork that is in the public domain. Dover Publications publishes books with copyright-free images for use by artists.

In this chapter, I will cover some easy and fun projects with your digital images. I used an Epson 1900 to print all of my digital images. I would like to thank Epson for their support and kindness.

CREATING DIGITAL IMAGES ON FABRIC WITH LARGE PRINTING LABELS

I use full-sized inkjet labels from the office-supply store to back fabric in order to stiffen it for use in a printer. In the United States the label size is 8½" x 11". The size varies in other countries. I find that the labels can be used over and over and are less likely to jam the printer than freezer paper used for the same purpose. I can get about four or five prints from one inkjet label. This process works well on cotton. Muslin fabric with white patterns screened onto the surface make especially interesting prints. You can also use light colors of fabric, silk, rayon, and satins. Experiment!

1. Cut a piece of fabric to the size of the inkjet label, if possible. Peel back a portion of the label backing and place the top edge of the fabric on the sticky part of the label. Peel more of the backing paper off and press a little more fabric onto the label. Continue until the fabric completely covers the sticky side of the label.

   If the fabric does not completely cover the entire sticky surface of the label, apply additional fabric strips to the remaining areas of adhesive, butting the edges of the fabric together and taking care not to overlap the fabrics. Be sure to trim off any loose threads.

2. Place the backing paper from the label on top of the fabric and use a bone folder to smooth over the surface to ensure the fabrics are secured to the label. Save the backing paper for use in step 4.

3. Print a digital image onto the adhesive backed fabric.

4. Remove the fabric from the label. Put the backing paper back on the label so that you can use the label to make further prints.

5. Use an iron to press the print between two Teflon pressing sheets.

6. If your printer inks are not permanent, they will bleed if they become wet; therefore they will need to be coated to preserve the colors and prevent bleeding. If using nonpermanent inks, let the image set for one to two days, and then coat it with a thin coating of light matte or gloss medium. Pour the medium into a flat dish and use a large brush to apply the medium to the surface. If you coat the piece immediately, there is a chance that the inks will bleed.

I am fascinated by the sculpture of Benin, Nigeria. My favorite piece is an ancient ivory mask displayed in the British Museum. I took a photograph of the piece and played with the photo in Paint Shop Pro on my computer. I altered the color, texture, and background of the mask and then printed the image onto muslin that had white stars silk-screened on the surface.

I used the same photo in the composition at right. First, I used software to add color to the photo. Then I printed the image at one end of a long piece of cotton fabric that had a paper backing. I reduced the image on my computer and printed it at the opposite end of the fabric, so that the masks would appear one above the other. Printing with nonpermanent inks allowed me to spray the images with water to make the colors run. I added paint, colored pencil, and some machine stitching to complete the design.

GALLERY

I started this piece at a shop in England called Rainbow Silks when I was teaching a digital-image class there. I printed two digital images on Jacquard inkjet cotton and then sewed the two images together to create the background. The appliqués are a mix of painted fabric and other inkjet-printed images and are sewn in place with variegated thread. Short pieces of fabric cord were added over two of the digital-image appliqués.

In this piece, digital images were inkjet printed onto cotton and ExtravOrganza from Jacquard. Painted fabrics were added to the printed ones, and the entire piece was embellished with seed beads, leaf beads, textured yarn, and decorative sewing, both by hand and by machine.

The digital image that is the focal point of this composition is from a photo I took of a prehistoric statue in the British Museum. I altered the colors and textures in Paint Shop Pro and printed the image onto fabric. I then cut out the image and used both the positive and negative pieces, overlapping them and machine stitching them in place. The background is comprised of several different fabrics stitched together using a variety of decorative and straight stitches. For added color and texture, I appliquéd pieces of a sheer gold scarf, couched on cords, and added more machine stitching. I like the shaped lower edge of the design because it's so different from what I usually do.

Here's a simple way to create an interesting effect: let the fabric do the work. The image is a photograph of a bas-relief that I took at the British Museum. It's printed on muslin that had a white grid silk-screened over the surface. The white grids show up as texture behind the photographic image.

GALLERY

This long panel is made up of five different painted and stamped fabric pieces stitched together. After the panel was assembled, I printed images on cotton and appliquéd them; then I added layers of Jacquard ExtravOrganza here and there, some sewn on by hand and some by machine. The beauty of the ExtravOrganza is that it's transparent and allows images on previous layers to show through. The picture of the little girl is me at age six. I like the expression on my face. I look like I have an important secret that I'm keeping.

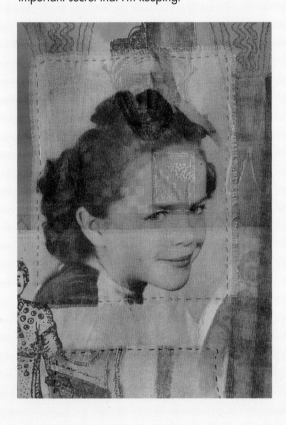

Facing page: I loved creating this design. It evolved over many years as I experimented with different techniques and colors. It features a variety of painted and rubber-stamped images and is layered with inkjet-printed fabrics, commercial fabrics, beads, textured yarn, and dyed facial wipes. There are areas of hand and machine stitching. I even tried my hand at free-motion machine embroidery in two areas.

Inkjet labels were used twice in this fabric-based design. First, they were torn and used as a resist when creating the painted background. Then, because painting over the labels made them decorative as well, I let them dry, tore them into pieces, and stitched three of them onto the background. Narrow lines of zigzag and decorative stitching further enhance the piece.

Inkjet Labels

Inkjet labels from your local office supply store can be torn or cut to use as a resist on fabric. They can be sent through a copier to make collage pieces for creating with paper. They can be painted or colored with almost any media. Here are some of the projects you can try.

INKJET LABELS AS A RESIST ON FABRIC

1. Cut or tear labels into the desired size and shape. Apply the label pieces to a previously painted background fabric, colored fabric, or white fabric, and press the label pieces firmly into place. A creative brayer design was used here. See pages 55–57. Injket labels will adhere to paper, so they will not work as a resist on paper.

2. Apply paint over the fabric and labels by rubber stamping or sponging.

3. Paint until satisfied with the design, and then remove the labels to reveal the patterns created.

USING INKJET LABELS IN COLLAGES

1. Copy or print digital family photos or other images (I used a digital image of a piece of artwork) onto a full-sized inkjet label. Remove an inkjet label from the backing paper. Cut or tear the inkjet label into the desired shapes, and then place them onto the backing paper temporarily.

2. Place the inkjet label pieces onto the chosen background surface and press firmly in place with a bone folder. The surface can be prepainted if desired. Reserve any remaining label pieces on the protective backing paper and place in a sheet protector for future use.

3. If desired add more paint to the design. If the labels contrast sharply with the background, you can paint over them with Jacquard Textile Traditionals to soften the images.

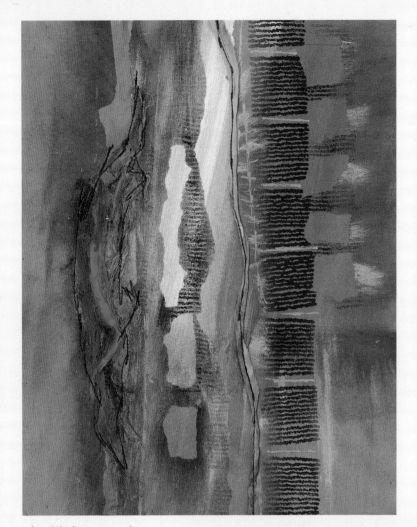

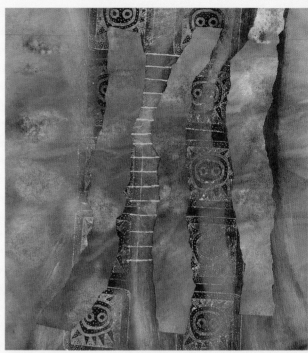

To make this piece, I applied long strips torn from an inkjet label to a painted yellow-and-ochre background; then I painted and rubber-stamped over and around the strips. After removing the strips, I used applicator-tipped paint to create horizontal lines.

Inkjet labels were used as a resist in this piece that also includes dyed and appliquéd facial wipes and a long, thin fabric cord. The background is painted fabric with rubber stamping.

This began with a photograph of my parents printed onto an inkjet label, trimmed to size, and applied to a heavy piece of Bristol board. I glazed the faces with Jacquard Textile Traditionals for an antiqued look, then applied many layers of paint to add richness and depth. The patterned strip on the left side was made using a triangle-patterned rubber stamp and Delta letter stencils that I sponged around. I glued two pieces of heavy fabric cord, a piece of stamped and painted air-dry clay, and a piece of painted fabric to the surface, again on the left. On the right, I added an embossed paper strip and three small rectangles made with the Cuttlebug.

An early photograph of my mother is the focal point of this collage. I printed the photo onto an inkjet label and tore irregular edges. I placed the label on a sheet of illustration board and glazed the image with Jacquard Textile Traditionals. I used gesso to texture the surface around the photo and other selected areas. I painted areas, and then wiped the paint away to create an aged look. I layered color, gesso, rubber stamping, and more paint until I was satisfied. To finish, I added a painted strip of paper embossed with circular motifs made with the Cuttlebug.

This is a photo of me as a baby, printed onto an inkjet label and applied to a heavy Bristol board. I glazed the picture with light layers of Jacquard Textile Traditionals, using a sponge with most of the color removed for even more transparency. The background was sponge painted and rubber stamped. The lines on each side of the baby picture are metallic paint added with an applicator tip.

For this piece, I cut long rectangles from a foam sheet and glued them to a piece of cardboard to make a stamp. With a ballpoint pen, I etched lines into the rectangles, pressing very hard with the pen so that the marked lines would show when I did the stamping. I applied different values of black and charcoal paint to the stamp and stamped the color onto a piece of white cotton fabric, then added other colors with a brush.

FOAM STAMPS

Children's hobby foam sheets with an adhesive back make ideal stamps. The sheets can be cut easily into a variety of shapes and can be glued to cardboard pieces cut from heavy corrugated cartons. Both sides of the cardboard can have foam shapes glued to it so the stamps take up less storage space. The foam accepts any water-based paint and the stamps can be printed on any absorbent surface.

MAKING STAMPS FROM FOAM SHEETS

1. Draw the desired stamp shape onto the front side of an adhesive-backed foam sheet with a ballpoint pen. Cut it out with a pair of scissors.

2. Peel the protective sheet from the foam shape. Press the adhesive side of the shape onto a piece of cardboard, creating a foam stamp. Repeat with any additional shapes as desired. When finished, trim off any excess cardboard.

3. If desired, score lines onto the foam shape with a ballpoint pen.

4. Apply paint to a sponge square and pat paint onto the foam stamp.

5. Press the painted foam image against the chosen background.

6. Lift off the foam stamp and repeat the stamping process using additional paint colors as desired.

GALLERY

This piece was created with three different foam stamps that I made. I started by stamping the abstract figure onto a piece of fabric that was already painted, then stamped a circle above and a pattern of repeating triangles across the bottom. Colored pencil adds highlights.

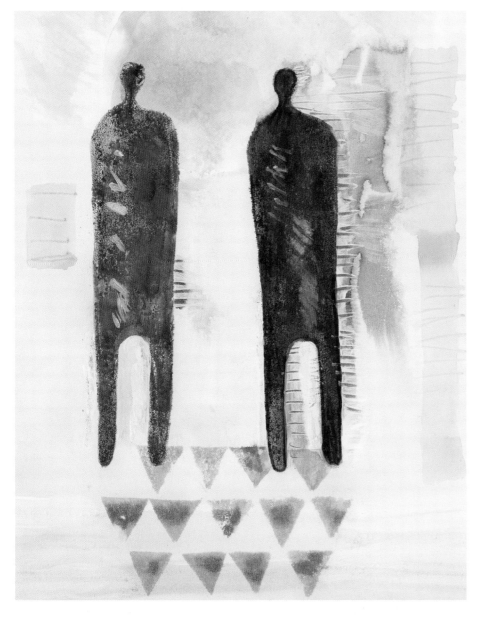

Abstract figures and repeating triangles were used again here, this time with very different results. I stamped the two figures onto painted heavyweight cardstock using very wet paint. I added gesso around them, and then scratched into the wet gesso with the end of my brush. I also drew lines on the gesso with a water-soluble pencil.

The foam stamp used on this piece was made up of many small rectangles and triangles cut from adhesive-backed foam and adhered to a piece of cardboard. I sponged color onto the stamp and repeatedly stamped across a piece of cardstock. When the stamped images were dry, I diluted paint and sponged a wash over the entire design.

I used the repeating triangle motif again in the piece at left, this time as the primary design element. A painted fabric background was heavily stamped in two areas using a foam stamp with a series of triangles. After stamping, I added more paint to the piece, and then used a small brush to outline selected triangles, darken some, and lighten others. I used the same small brush to add a few curvy lines.

This is my most complex stencil design and the first one I did with playing-card stencils. I started on a piece of heavy white cardstock and stenciled the figure in two places, using orange paint. I added the third figure by holding the stencil cutout firmly in place with my fingers and using a battery-operated toothbrush to apply the paint to the background around the figure. I built layers of paint and stencils then added colored-pencil work.

STENCILS

I found a deck of large playing cards at a dollar store in Victoria, British Columbia, while teaching there. I immediately thought of using the playing cards for stencils. I figured they were strong enough, water resistant, and would be easy to cut with a sharp craft knife. I used some of my own rubber stamp designs as inspiration. You can also cut stencils from manila folders, cardboard take-out container lids, or template plastic. Be sure to keep both the stencil and the piece that was cut from it. Sometimes using both the negative and positive design is just what you need to create an exciting piece. Try using more than one stencil in a composition or turn the stencil over and make a mirror image. Also try overlapping stencil designs.

MAKING STENCILS

1. Draw a design onto the chosen stencil material using a permanent marker. You may want to practice on paper first.

2. Place the stencil material on a self-healing cutting mat and cut out the design with a sharp craft knife.

3. After making the stencil, place it on the chosen design surface. The surface can be previously painted if desired. Put some paint onto a paint palette, dip a battery-operated toothbrush into the paint, and then brush the excess off onto the palette. If the paint is too heavy, it will creep under the stencil design and make fuzzy edges in your design. Apply the paint through the stencil opening using the toothbrush.

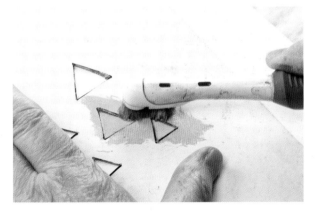

4. Use another stencil if desired and stencil more images to other areas of the design surface. Continue until satisfied with the results.

GALLERY

These four small paintings started as one large piece of artwork. Something told me they'd be more interesting cut into four designs and developed individually. I'm very pleased with the results.

This is a wonderful example of the complex effects
you can achieve when you layer stencil over
stencil and color over color. I combined several
different stencils here, including a spiral, a bird, and
triangles, then enhanced the designs with colored
pencils in a variety of colors.

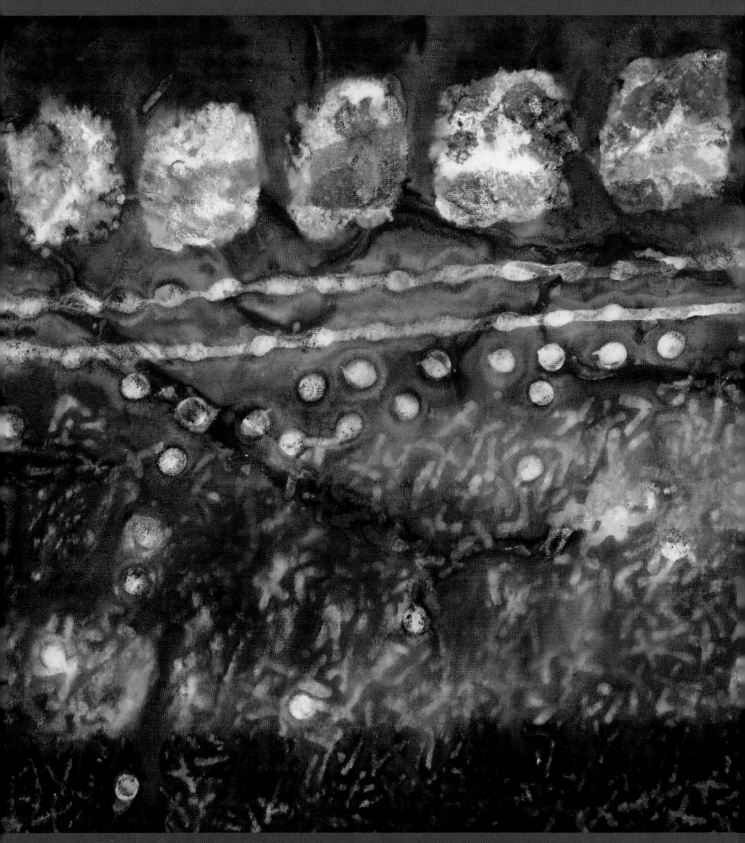

Thick hair gel was sponged and painted onto silk habotai, which was then sprayed with water and dyed with Dye-na-Flow applied with eyedroppers.

HAIR-GEL RESIST

Through experimentation, I've learned that inexpensive hair gel acts as a wonderful resist. In addition, I've learned that it can be added to paint to make it slick and easy to scrape and layer. I've worked on different surfaces and love the effects that can be achieved. Experiment with different hair gels and see if there are differences in the final effect. The resist technique can be done with Dye-na-Flow or other liquid paint, dye, or ink. Be sure to cover the work surface with plastic to prevent staining. Wearing rubber gloves is also recommended.

STAMPED HAIR-GEL DESIGNS

1. Place a piece of paper or fabric onto a plastic-covered work surface. If using silk or cotton, you can do two pieces at the same time since the dye will soak through to the bottom layer.

2. Tap a sponge square into hair gel applied to a freezer-paper palette. Sponge the hair gel onto a rubber stamp.

3. Turn the stamp over onto the design surface and press firmly on the back of the stamp. Carefully lift the stamp off the surface.

4. Spray the surface with a fine-mist spray bottle filled with water.

5. Use an applicator-tipped bottle or an eyedropper to apply liquid paint, dye, or ink over the surface and let the hair gel resist the paint.

6. Repeat step 5 with additional dye colors. Use a sponge square to pat the color onto any bare area until satisfied with the results. If you have lots of paint on the design surface you may choose to do a print at this time. See "Making Hair-Gel Resist Prints" (page 93). Or, finish as in step 7 on page 92.

7. Let the finished piece dry. If you are working on fabric, let the fabric dry completely, and then heat set the paint following the manufacturer's instructions. When the fabric was dry, I added colored pencil to this sample.

SPONGED HAIR GEL

1. Place a piece of paper or fabric onto a plastic-covered work surface. If using silk or cotton, you can do two pieces at the same time since the dye will soak through to the bottom layer.

2. Apply hair gel to a sponge by squeezing the hair gel into the sponge or by tapping a sponge into hair gel applied to a palette. Sponge the hair gel onto the chosen surface. If desired, scrape through the gel with a scraping tool, such as a comb or plastic knife.

3. Spray the surface with a fine-mist spray bottle filled with water.

4. Use an applicator-tipped bottle or an eye-dropper to apply liquid paint, dye, or ink over the surface and let the hair gel resist the paint.

5. Use a sponge to move paint to any bare areas. Apply additional paint colors and sponge the paint over the surface until satisfied with the results. If you have lots of paint on the design surface you may choose to do a print at this time. See "Making Hair-Gel Resist Prints" (page 93). Or, finish as in step 6 below.

6. Let the finished piece dry. If you are working on fabric, let the fabric dry completely, and then heat set the paint according to the manufacturer's instructions.

MAKING HAIR-GEL RESIST PRINTS

1. Create a stamped or sponged hair-gel design following the methods on pages 91 and 92.

2. Place a piece of paper over a sponged or stamped hair-gel resist design while still wet.

3. Roll a brayer over every portion of the paper.

4. Remove the paper to reveal the hair-gel designs. You'll have two painted designs: the original painting with hair gel and the print created by using the brayer.

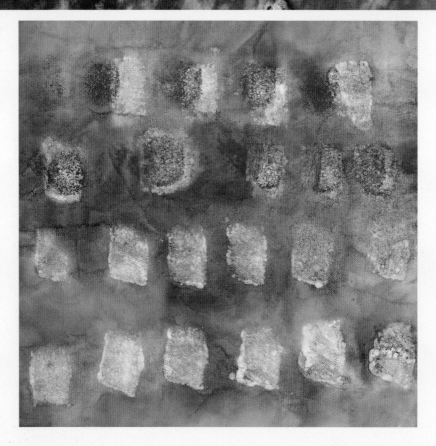

I used Golden Yellow-, True Red-, and Fuchsia-colored Dye-na-Flow on cotton to create the sample shown. The light-colored areas are where the hair gel was sponged onto the surface and resisted the paint. I sponged Violet-colored Neopaque in areas to finish the piece. The back of the piece, shown below, is more subtle but equally beautiful, and could be used instead of the front.

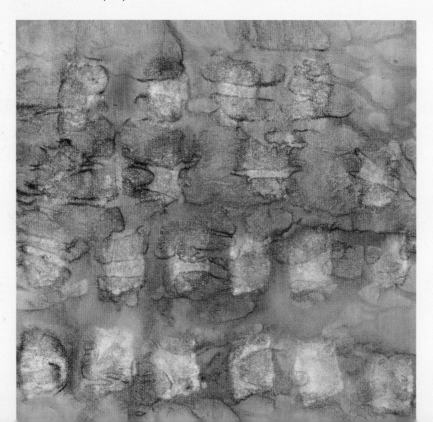

This silk piece was sponged with hair gel and dyed with only two Dye-na-Flow colors—Violet and Golden Yellow. The colors mixed to form the browns and ochres.

This heavy cardstock design began with hair gel and light aqua paint applied to the surface and scraped with a plastic knife to create texture. Violet-colored Dye-na-Flow applied with an eyedropper bled into the scraped areas. I was able to make a print of the original with a second piece of heavy cardstock.

A piece of cotton fabric was the base for this design. It was sponged with hair gel and then scraped with a plastic knife to make linear patterns. Dye-na-Flow applied to the surface bled into the linear patterns.

Deep, vivid colors are the result of many successive glue and dye applications. To create greater contrast, I allowed some small areas of the white fabric to show.

WASHABLE GLUE BATIK

I love the effect of batik but don't want to melt hot wax or have to go through the elaborate steps needed to create it. I experimented with children's white and gel washable glues and found that I could make very interesting batiks with little or no effort. For this technique, use Dye-na-Flow or other liquid paint, dye, or permanent ink on silk or cotton. When using dyes, be sure to cover the work surface with plastic and wear protective gloves to prevent staining.

CREATING BATIK WITH GLUE

1. Place a piece of fabric onto a plastic-covered work surface or cover the surface with a large piece of freezer paper shiny side up. If working with silk or cotton, layer a second piece of fabric under the first piece to capture color that bleeds through.

2. Squeeze glue onto a sponge. Use the sponge to pat glue onto a rubber stamp. Apply the glue liberally to get a good image on the fabric.

3. Turn the stamp over and press onto the fabric.

4. Draw lines onto the fabric with the glue bottle and scrap through the lines with a scraping tool, such as a comb or plastic knife, as shown. You can also sponge the glue directly onto the surface if desired.

5. Mist the fabric with water using a fine-mist spray bottle. Apply Dye-na-Flow, liquid paint, or permanent ink to the fabric, using applicator-tipped bottles or an eyedropper. When doing your design, start with lighter colors and progressively use darker colors.

6. Use a sponge to pat the dye around and distribute color to the edges.

7. Let the dye dry completely, and then heat set the dyed fabric between two Teflon pressing sheets, following the manufacturer's instructions.

8. Remove the glue with a scrub brush and water in a sink.

9. Iron the wet piece until dry, and then repeat steps 2–4, covering selected areas of the design with more glue. Be sure to apply some glue to the lightest areas of the design in order to retain those colors after future dyeing processes with darker dyes.

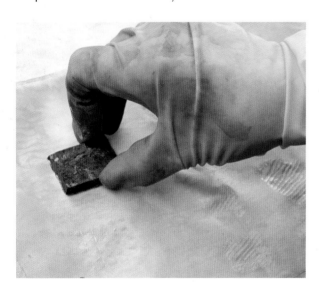

10. Continue as in steps 5 and 6 with a darker paint color.

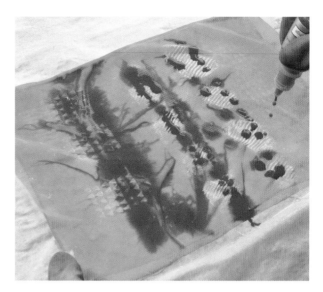

11. Continue as in steps 7 and 8. Heat set the final piece after it dries, following the manufacturer's instructions.

The samples above, below, and at left began with white silk. The strong patterns were created by applying glue to the design surface with rubber stamps. Each piece is the result of multiple glue-and-dye processes.

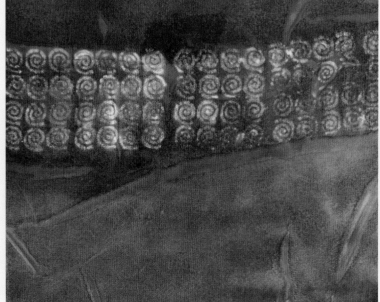

This sample began as white cotton. The glue-batik patterns were created by sponging, scraping, and rubber stamping. The layers of color were built up through successive glue-and-dye processes.

This print was created by masking off areas with copy paper and then applying paint to the open areas. I added paint and texture to the gelatin in layers, making a print each time until the entire piece was covered with paint. I then stamped more paint in a few areas and embellished with strips of painted fabric and a wavy fabric cord.

GELATIN PRINTING

Gelatin printing has been around for many years, but it took Rayna Gillman's book to make me want to try this. Thank you, Rayna. We have different styles of working, but her work inspired me to do the technique with my own style. You will find that the results will be different depending upon the paint that you use. I do this technique with Jacquard Versatex Printing and Jacquard Professional Grade Silk Screen inks. What is different about this technique versus other printing techniques is that the gelatin is flexible and you get very unusual prints. You can create patterns on the surface of the gelatin by pressing textural items, such as sequin waste, kitchen-sink mats, rubbing plates, or rubber stamps, into the paint and removing them before printing. You can print on rice paper, fabric, cardstock, leather, or any other absorbent surface. It's joyful to feel the surface of the gelatin and because it is malleable, the prints are very interesting. Use the print for the background of a design, tear it apart for use in other projects, or leave it as a finished piece of art.

GELATIN RECIPE

This recipe will give you a nice thick, flexible surface that can be used over and over again for printing.
- 8 envelopes of unflavored gelatin
- 2 cups of boiling water
- 2 cups of cool water

Mix the cool water and gelatin together in a 9" x 9" disposable aluminum pan until the gelatin is dissolved. Add the boiling water and stir until all of the bubbles are gone. Put the mixture in the refrigerator to harden. The gelatin should be set and ready for printing the next day. When set, turn the gelatin over onto a serving tray that is at least two inches larger than the gelatin all around. Removing the gelatin from the pan will give you a larger printing area.

CREATING PRINTS WITH GELATIN

1. Apply paint to the gelatin with any of the following methods: brushing lightly, rubber stamping images, sponging, patting it on with rags, or any other method you can devise to get paint onto the surface. Use care when applying paint to the gelatin surface because it can be scarred or fractured if you put too much pressure on it. (Of course, you may want to gouge the surface to create a design. In that case, any blunt or sharp tool will do.) To print your fabric or paper right now, go on to step three.

2. While the paint is wet, press different textures into the paint such as sequin waste, shower-mat pieces, kitchen mats, slotted wooden forks, kitchen items with texture, grids, rubber stamps, or textured plastic placemats. Then remove the textural items to reveal a pattern in the paint.

3. When satisfied with the painted gelatin, lay a piece of fabric or paper onto the painted gelatin surface and press firmly with your fingers across the back.

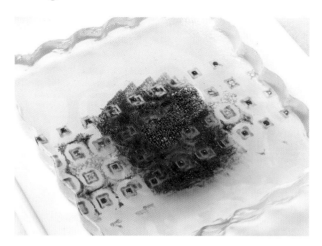

4. Carefully remove the fabric and turn right side up to reveal the design. The sample shown below includes an intriguing grouping of circles caused by bubbles on the surface of the gelatin.

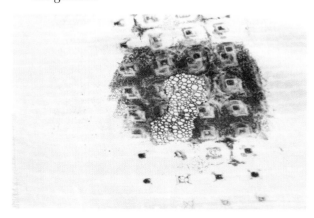

5. Repeat steps 1–4 as many times as necessary until satisfied with the results.

6. After printing for the day, cover the gelatin on the tray with plastic wrap and put it back in the refrigerator to use again. Eventually the gelatin will start cracking and the cracks will give you interesting results. Remember, you can also gouge into the surface with a knife or other tools to create patterns.

7. For prints on fabric, heat set the fabric according to the manufacturer's instructions.

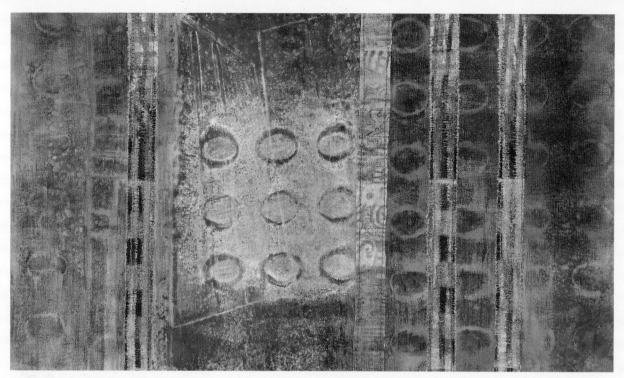

The background of this piece was created by patting color on the gelatin and then pressing a rubber kitchen mat into the surface. I did several overlays of color with successive prints. For additional color and texture, I appliquéd several previously painted strips of fabric to the piece.

Repeatedly rubber stamping images onto the gelatin surface with different colors of paint produced the highly patterned background shown here. On this piece, too, I appliquéd a series of previously painted fabric pieces to the printed background.

White printed muslin was the starting point for this gelatin print. I sponged and rubber-stamped on the gelatin to produce patterns, which I then printed onto the muslin. To complete the design, I appliquéd a painted-fabric rectangle to the right side of the composition and stitched three narrow fabric strips to the left side using a machine decorative stitch and variegated thread.

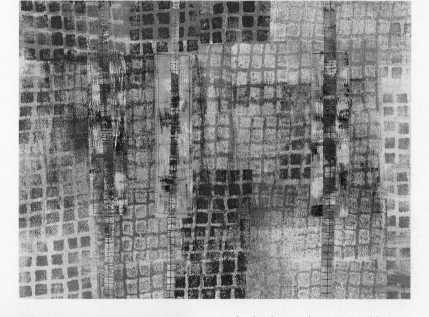

This is the first gelatin print I made. I love that it turned out so painterly. I experimented with bubble wrap to create some of the circles and did a series of rubber-stamped impressions on the wet paint. To finish the piece I appliquéd two contrasting strips of fabric to the surface.

This background was created by a series of rubber-stamped impressions in wet paint on gelatin, which was then printed onto white fabric. I did a progression of prints to build up the colors. The piece is embellished with three painted fabric rectangles topped by three long, narrow fabric strips, all appliquéd in place with decorative machine stitching and variegated thread.

Dorland's Wax Medium was mixed with acrylic paint to create this design on heavy cardstock. I layered many colors to achieve the depth.

DORLAND'S WAX MEDIUM

Dorland's Wax Medium from Jacquard has been used by artists for years. It comes in a jar and is often heated to a liquid form to use as a coating over artwork. The label on the jar also describes adding the wax to a variety of paints and dried powders, so I mixed pigment with the wax and painted on cardstock and fabric. It will work on all fabrics. I love the painterly effects that I achieve by using the wax with my paints. The wax helps the paint stay workable and slows the drying time. After the paint dries, I iron it between two Teflon pressing sheets. The finished effect varies depending on the painting surface used. I think you will enjoy experimenting with this product.

PAINTING WITH DORLAND'S WAX MEDIUM

1. Squeeze paint onto the palette. Dip a brush into the wax medium and mix with the paint on the palette.

2. Apply the paint-and-wax mixture to the selected design surface. You will notice that the paint does not completely mix with the wax, so the brush strokes are very textured.

3. Use a scraping tool, such as a plastic knife, the end of a brush, or any other scraping tool to scrape through the paint.

4. Continue to apply additional paint colors mixed with wax and to use scraping tools as desired until satisfied with the results. Let the painting dry.

5. After the paint and wax have dried, cover the painting with a piece of copy paper, and then it between two Teflon ironing sheets. Set the iron to "no steam" and the hottest setting and press over the top Teflon sheet. This process will heat set the paint and the wax and transfer some color to the copy paper. Save the copy paper for use in future projects.

PAINTING WITH DORLAND'S WAX MEDIUM ON A HEATED GRIDDLE

1. Cover an electric griddle with heavy-duty aluminum foil. Heat the electric griddle to 175°. Place a piece of paper onto the foil-covered griddle.

2. Dip your brush into the wax medium and apply the wax to the paper. Squeeze paint onto the paper. Hold the paper in place with a wooden spatula and mix the paint with the wax using a paintbrush. An alternative is to mix the paint and wax on freezer paper before applying the color to the design surface.

3. Continue to add paint and wax as desired.

BE CAREFUL

This technique is done with an electric griddle and is not for children. They could easily burn themselves. Do not heat the griddle so hot that it smokes.

4. Use a comb, a plastic knife, the end of a brush, a cut-up credit card, or any other scraping tool to scrape through the paint to the surface below. You will create rich textures on your painting by repeating this process.

5. Repeat steps 2–4 as needed until satisfied with the results.

6. After the paint and wax have dried, cover the painting with a piece of copy paper, and then place it between two Teflon ironing sheets. Set the iron to "no steam" and the hottest setting and press over the top Teflon sheet. This process will heat set the paint and the wax.

7. If desired, add metallic paint accents or other acrylics by brush, without wax, to highlight selected areas. Heat set the paint again when finished.

For these two pieces, I mixed acrylics with Dorland's Wax Medium and layered many colors to achieve greater depth. Scratching through layers of paint revealed the colors below.

Habotai silk was the base for this painting. After heat setting the artwork, I added metallic paint to the surface and scratched through the wet paint with the hard end of a brush.

For this piece, I applied layers of paint and wax to white cotton fabric. After heat setting the piece, I painted metallic highlights at selected areas.

A faded inkjet image was the starting point for this design. I added wax and pigment in layers over the printed image to create a rich effect.

RESOURCES

Corel
www.corel.com
Paint Shop Pro and photo-editing software

Epson
www.epson.com
Printers and ink

Golden Artist Colors, Inc.
www.goldenpaints.com
Matte medium

Gütermann of America
www.gutermann.com
Sewing thread

Janome America, Inc.
www.janome.com
Sewing machines for paper and fabric

Picasa 3
www.download.com

Provo Craft
www.provocraft.com
Cuttlebug and accessories

Ranger Industries
www.rangerink.com
Stamping and painting accessories, bone folders, brayers, and Teflon pressing sheets

Rupert, Gibbon & Spider
(Jacquard Products)
www.jacquardproducts.com
Neopaque, Lumiere, Dye-na-Flow, Textile Traditionals, Versatex Screen Printing Inks, Jacquard Airbrush Colors, Dorland's Wax Medium, ExtravOrganza, Silk Salt, and applicator-tipped bottles and applicator tips

Sargent Art
www.sargentart.com
Gesso, mediums, and paint

Impress Me Rubber Stamp Company
Sherrill Kahn
17116 Escalon Drive
Encino, CA 91436-4030
Telephone/Fax: (818) 788-6730
www.impressmenow.com
Catalog: $5.00, refundable with a coupon
Rubber stamps and Sherrill Kahn's books

Strathmore Artist Papers
www.strathmoreartist.com
Bristol board and papers

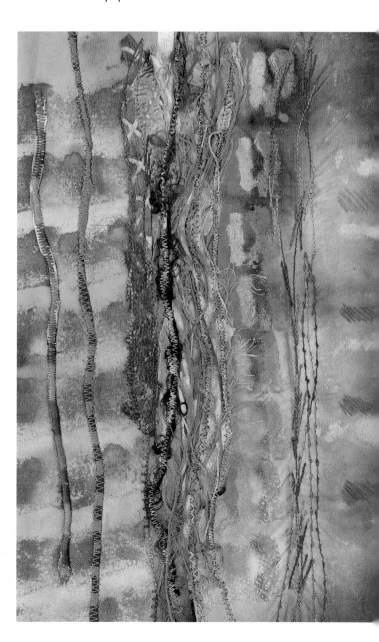

ABOUT THE AUTHOR

Sherrill was an art educator for 30 years in the public schools; her focus was on drawing, painting, fiber, and design. Since her retirement, she has taught nationally and internationally for stores, conferences, guilds, and educational institutions. Sherrill owns Impress Me, a rubber-stamp company, with her husband, Joel. She has designed six fabric lines with Robert Kaufman and has written numerous magazine articles. This is her sixth book.

Sherrill has loved to draw and paint as long as she can remember. She would sit for hours coloring and painting as a young girl. Her mother, Ann, who taught elementary school, taught her to sew, knit, and crochet.

Today Sherrill continues to experiment with every possible media. She loves to play endlessly with her designs on the computer, as well as draw, knit, crochet, make fused glass, and create three-dimensional pieces. Sherrill enjoys trying out every new product that seems interesting. She definitely lives by the words "What if?" and hopes you enjoy and have fun with the techniques in *Creative Mixed Media*.

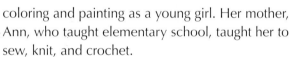

MORE ONLINE!

- Visit www.impressmenow.com to see more of Sherrill Kahn's work and to find her teaching schedule.

- Go to www.martingale-pub.com to learn more about Sherrill's books.